'Reading just one ... playwriting is the worst thing a p... reading none. Li... Fraser Grace, Conve... dies, University of Birmingham'

'At last…a book about writing for writers, by someone who is a writer and understands the writing process. This is now my favourite book about writing. Better than any of those expensive writing courses.'
In-Sook Chappell, winner of 2007 Verity Bargate Award

'This is truly liberating for any writer who is "stuck" or struggling with the "rules" one is told to adhere to in conventional writers handbooks. The quotes are inspiring, the exercises useful and imaginative, and Lisa Goldman's experience and insight supportive and spot on. This book makes writing magical and exciting again. A breath of fresh air.'
Natasha Langridge, winner of 2010 Meyer-Whitworth Award

'This is an absolutely fantastic book which I highly recommend for anyone who is passionate about playwriting – whether they are playwrights, directors or, like me, literary managers and dramaturgs. Drawing on Lisa's vast experience of developing plays for the stage, it's comprehensive, playful and inspiring – revealing the rules and then revisiting them from surprising angles and vivid reference points. Great stuff.'
Sarah Dickinson, dramaturg (Soho Theatre)

'The writing process can be an overwhelming task. Lisa Goldman, however, challenges her readers to create their own set of principles as they put pen to paper. Goldman's approach is fresh and interesting, showing pros and cons, explaining the rationale behind following and breaking each rule. Writers who need a fresh approach and are willing to be challenged will find plenty of ideas to explore in *The No Rules Handbook for Writers.*'
The Writer's Journey

'Love the book! A genuinely welcome alternative to all the navel-gazing "How to…" books.'
Paul Sirett, multi-award-winning playwright and ex-dramaturg of RSC

'Written by someone who truly cares about the writer's process. Right up there with Truby and McKee.'
Simon Allen, casting director, actors' agent and screenwriter

'Full of sensible advice'
Lyn Gardner, Guardian

'An invitation to writers, both new and established, to join in with a literary form of civil disobedience. Where McKee's structuralist prescriptions do the writer's thinking for her, Goldman puts her at the centre of an agile, dynamic thought process. While remaining free of bombast, this is an authoritative piece. Goldman has been responsible for developing a dizzying array of important new work… Neither does she neglect the bigger picture: the point of being a writer. A section entitled 'Principles of freedom' offers a powerful vision of the writer's role. Her reference to Iranian film-maker Jafar Panahi, under house arrest and being "accused of the thought-crime of imagining a film about the post-election demonstrations", is particularly moving.'
Simon Turley, playwright, The Weekly Worker

'It's going up on my bookshelf up alongside the essential reads…this book is a treasure trove of advice, and one I hope will be in print for many years to come. You've done writers around the world proud.'
Mohsen Shah, playwright

'An easy to read, funny, straightforward, sensible and inspirational book for writers at all stages of their career. Read it right through and continue to dip in and out. I don't like/read books about writing or acting. This no rules handbook broke that rule, for me.'
Terri-Ann Brumby, writer and actor

'Feisty, helpful, liberating stuff'
The Stage

'What emerges is the primacy of the writer's unique voice, a voice that Goldman seeks to liberate rather than stifle. She expands on various approaches to writing, setting forth helpful tips and exercises, but continually emphasises that each writer should go with what works for them. It is a refreshing approach that quite rightly places the writer as individual at its centre.'
The Public Reviews

'Much of what makes the book so useful is that it draws on the experience of actual working writers. Goldman herself is a well-established figure in theatre, so she is used to working with, and commissioning writers, and knows both how writers function and what audiences respond to.'
Exeunt Magazine

the

NO
RULES

handbook for writers

(know the rules so you can break them)

Lisa Goldman

OBERON BOOKS
LONDON
WWW.OBERONBOOKS.COM

First published in 2012 by Oberon Books Ltd
521 Caledonian Road, London N7 9RH
Tel: +44 (0) 20 7607 3637 / Fax: +44 (0) 20 7607 3629
e-mail: info@oberonbooks.com
www.oberonbooks.com

A catalogue record for this book is available from the British Library.

PB ISBN: 978-1-84943-111-8
EPUB: 978-1-84943-301-3

Cover design by James Illman

Cartoons by Eleanor Pletts

Printed and bound by CPI Group (UK) Ltd, Croydon, CR0 4YY.

Visit www.oberonbooks.com to read more about all our books and to buy them. You will also find features, author interviews and news of any author events, and you can sign up for e-newsletters so that you're always first to hear about our new releases.

Acknowledgements

Special thanks to friends and family who read bits of this book at different stages for your encouraging and helpful comments: John Chamberlain, Jan Goldman, Natasha Langridge, Tania Rodrigues and Mohsen Shah. Big thanks to Mohsen again and to Kester Aspden, Ishia Bennison, Mike Dormer and Sara Murray for your generosity in introducing me to some wonderful novelists and screenwriters. Thanks to Noma Dumezweni, Simon Allen, Ben Whishaw for kindness and to Greg Doran for thoughts about Shakespeare and 5-Act Structure. Thank you to Eleanor Pletts for drawing gorgeous cartoons and to Donna Westall for introducing us. Thanks to all at Oberon Books for your cleverness, patience and hospitality. In particular to James Hogan for commissioning, Andrew Walby and Melina Theocharidou for editing, James Illman for design and Lewis Morgan for marketing. Thanks to Emma Schad and Lisa Gee for PR chats and to my lovely agent Julia Tyrrell. Special thanks to Aleks Sierz for reading and endorsing. Huge thanks again to all rule breaking writers, quoted or not, who have helped to make this book what it is.

Rule /rool/ n. that which is normal or usual; conformity to good or established usage; a guiding principle; a standard; a convention; a maxim or formula; control.

'**integrity has no need of rules**'
Albert Camus, *The Myth of Sisyphus*[1]

About the Author

Lisa Goldman is a leading director, dramaturg and producer of new plays. For fifteen years she was Artistic Director of two new writing companies, the Red Room, which she founded, and more recently Soho Theatre. Work she developed has won or been nominated for all major UK playwriting awards. Plays include *Inheritance* by Mike Packer; *Baghdad Wedding* by Hassan Abdulrazzak (Meyer Whitworth and George Devine Awards 2008); *Behud* by Gurpreet Kaur Bhatti; *The Bogus Woman* (Scotsman Fringe First and MEN Award, finalist Susan Smith Blackburn), *Animal* and *Bites* by Kay Adshead; *Shraddhā* by Natasha Langridge (Meyer Whitworth Award 2010); *The Censor* (Time Out Live Award; Writers Guild Best Play 1997) and *Stitching* (Time Out Live Award 2003; Stage Award; Herald Angel Award; runner-up Evening Standard Award) by Anthony Neilson; *Iya Ile* by Oladipo Agboluaje (Alfred Fagon Award; runner-up Olivier Award 2010); *This Isn't Romance* by In-Sook Chappell (Verity Bargate Award 2007); *Pure Gold* by Michael Bhim; *Sunspots, The Shorewatcher's House* and *Know Your Rights* by Judy Upton; *Leaves of Glass* and *Piranha Heights* by Philip Ridley; *Made in England* by Parv Bancil; *A Day at the Racists* by Anders Lustgarten (inaugural Harold Pinter Award 2011); *Hoxton Story* which Lisa also wrote; and *A Couple of Poor Polish Speaking Romanians* by Dorota Maslowska which she co-translated with Paul Sirett. Lisa also runs masterclasses for writers in the UK and internationally. See www.lisagoldman.co.uk. You can contact Lisa at noruleshandbook@gmail.com or her agent Julia Tyrrell at julia@jtmanagement.co.uk.

Contributing Writers

Many brilliant writers have contributed their insights to this book. They are mostly based in the UK and write plays, screenplays, TV and radio drama, novels and Live Art. Some are emerging voices, others have half a century of experience and success behind them. They are all acclaimed writers and most have won major awards for their work. All are innovators and a few are infamous rule breakers. They are:

Hassan Abdulrazzak, Oladipo Agboluaje, Rachel Anthony,
Steve Bailie, Ronan Bennett, Gurpreet Kaur Bhatti,
Stephen Brady, Sita Brahmachari, Laura Bridgeman,
Trevor Byrne, Anthony Cartwright, In-Sook Chappell,
Greg Dinner, Matt Greenhalgh, Tanika Gupta,
David Hermanstein, Terry Hodgkinson, Lisa Holdsworth,
Amanda Holiday, M.J. Hyland, Dennis Kelly,
Bryony Lavery, Chris Lunt, Stacy Makishi,
Neel Mukherjee, Hattie Naylor, Anthony Neilson,
Kim Noble, Maysoon Pachachi, Chris Paling,
Tom Palmer, Penny Pepper, Lucy Prebble, Philip Ridley,
Paul Sirett, Paula B. Stanic, Edmund White,
Roy Williams, Rob Young, Justin Young.

If you don't know their works, I have listed a few titles at the end of this book. I cannot recommend them highly enough.

Is The No Rules Handbook for me?

I have designed this book to appeal to a new and hungry kind of writer – the original storyteller who writes for more than one medium. Specifically I had in mind the hundreds of playwrights I've worked with, all of whom also write TV drama, films or novels. Whatever mediums you work in, I hope that you will find something of use here. This is also a book for those who work with writers, such as teachers, workshop leaders, dramaturgs, editors, agents, producers and directors. Most of all this book aims to support and provoke the imaginations of those just starting out. You have already thrown away the rule book by taking the decision to write and although you may be new to writing you are not new to life, therefore this book doesn't patronize you or tell you what to do. I hope it does contribute in some small way to your creative journey in the world.

How to use this book

You can read this book cover to cover or dip into any rule, but do read the short introduction first. There is a shape and progression to the narrative but I also cross-reference rules to keep repetition to a minimum.

Style rules I break in this book

- I have used the term audience-reader and reader-audience, which isn't a word but feels easier on the eye than audience/reader.
- I use she or he interchangeably and only where that doesn't work do I use s/he.
- When Oberon Books commissioned this book, they asked me to discuss my experiences as a practitioner. Consequently, where possible I have cited plays that I've personally developed or directed and I offer my own experiences and perspectives. This makes for a drama bias in terms of references, though not in terms of rules. Writers' contributions balance this somewhat. To keep references to a minimum, whenever possible, I have mentioned the same book, film or play more than once.

CONTENTS: 40 Rules to be Broken

Conventions of Style, Economy and Consistency

Principles of Freedom:
Written and Unwritten Laws of Taste and Taboos

The Rules of Rewriting

The Writing Game:
Maxims of process and profession

Rules of being a Rule Breaker

Introduction: Rules or No Rules?

'You don't discover anything if you have a map. You've got to sail into the night and risk shipwrecks to find an island no one's seen before.'

Philip Ridley

This book is called *The No Rules Handbook for Writers* because there are no rules to writing except those you make and break as you write. Each writer's process is unique and the effort of others to perfect your writing can help improve your craft, but it may also discourage innovation. If it's possible to have an anti-handbook for writers I hope this is it.

I use the term 'rules' in a broad sense to mean principles, conventions and what is done 'as a rule.' Some rules are explicit, some are unspoken. You will find them in every guru-guide, writing workshop and notes session. This book questions why they exist and persist. I have deliberately chosen rules that are powerful and have currency in mainstream culture. We will explore their value as tools as well as how to bend and break them. Successful rule breaking also requires mastery. You will notice that some rules contradict each other; one person's rule is another's rule-breaker. As you write, you redefine what the rules are.

'It's been strange when I think of this subject of rule breaking. Because when I'm working I don't think I'm breaking rules. Even now, looking back on past work, it feels that in my world, in the context I, or the artist, create, nothing was rule breaking. What are these rules? It's others that tell me I am a rule breaker.'

Kim Noble, Live Artist

Your imagination is unruly. You don't focus on rules in the act of creation, let alone deliberately break them. When you are immersed in what's unfolding, you're flowing with the need of your fictional world. The subtle adjustment of trial and error is a practical application – a channeling of your wild vision. *Cut that beat. Open this emotional gap. Visualize it there in more detail. No, that's too on the nose! Meld those two moments into one – less is more.* These are all rules, but they underpin your sense of freedom. You follow feeling and instinct, obey the integrity of your vision. You call this 'what works.'

Of course what works for you, may not work for others. You become intrigued by the patterns of meaning that people see in your writing. You recognise that the conventions of 'good writing' or 'taste' exist in a political, psychological and cultural context. This is why producing work which breaks rules is riskier. One writer suggested to me, entirely without irony, that because of this, you should only break one rule at a time.

Mastery of rules is gained through a mixture of knowledge and practice. Experienced writers have an unconscious competence – they use conventions without thinking, and break rules freely. When you're starting out, you may struggle with these elements of craft. Rightly you're more concerned with questions of authentic voice and meaning. What you need in terms of craft starts with understanding yourself.

Screenwriter Stephen Brady explains:

> 'The more I write, the more it feels like that J.G. Ballard short story about the ever expanding ship; the more you explore, the more rooms you find and you realise the depth of your ignorance and the endless possibilities of form. At the beginning there was just one room, that of realism.'

Meaning is revealed through manipulation of form. As your voice becomes more confident, you explore new ways to express your world view. Your work becomes part of what new writers look to in order to learn the conventions of their craft. When you start work on a new project, your own imagination overturns or enriches these same conventions. The most important rules we break are our own – in art as in life. It is when we step outside of our comfort zone that we make the breakthroughs, because there we are confronted with the awkwardness of ourselves, the contradiction of who we are. There are no rules about who you can be when you write.

All great writing is an act of rebellion against what exists, a need to say something unsaid, an impossible attempt to heal what is broken, to make a mark. The freedom to express yourself through fiction is beautiful and thrilling; to speak about truths of the world you experience, to bestow on others the power to change their world.

> 'As a writer coming from the world of Live Art, I love making rules in order to break them. Sometimes new life and meaning can emerge between the cracks. Writing is strongest where something was once broken.'
>
> Stacy Makishi, Live Artist

Fiction enables us to hold contradictory thoughts and feelings as we experience them, to be inside multiple points of view. *The No Rules Handbook* is a book in argument with itself. No systems or schemas are promoted here, only provocations and practical ideas, exercises and writers' experiences. I hope some of them inspire you. In a space where there are no rules, nothing stands in the way of your impulse to imagine; your muse or whatever you want to call that wondrous process of creation and ceaseless incompletion.

RULES 1-7

The Practice of Preparation

They say there's all this stuff you must know before you start to write. Is it true? What do other writers do?

RULE 1

Write what you know

Like every rule in this book, **Write what you know** can be a useful tool. It is your unique, authentic perspective that creates interest in your work. So why not consciously delve into autobiography or draw on a distinct area of personal knowledge? Won't your work feel more truthful or even universal as a result? Writers have often freed their voices through this approach, basing their early works on personal experience.

Kim Noble, like many Live Artists, gives generously of his intimacy. In *Kim Noble Will Die* (2009) he offers pots of his ejaculate to women during the show, and projects his mum's head on a bucket talking about his failure.

Most writers feel too entwined in the material of their own lives to use it so self-consciously. You feel like your psyche would rebel – you'd self-censor or self-sabotage. Worse still, your family might never speak to you again.

Fictionalising people you know can be an emotionally tortuous process. In any case, the twisted complexity of real life has to be streamlined in a story. Awareness of your real-life models can also lead to blind spots in your writing. This is particularly true when the main character is modelled on yourself (see **Rules 14** and **16**). On the other hand, exquisite details, culled from your own discomfort, can elicit compassion from your reader-audience.

Writing what you know may also offer the potential for self-liberation. In her play *Behud* (2010), Gurpreet Kaur Bhatti fictionalised the experience of having her 2004 play *Behzti* censored. Kim Noble created *Kim Noble Will Die* following a suicidal breakdown. Sometimes as a writer you need to explore momentous true-life events through your work in order to move on. These pieces are discussed in more depth in **Rules 29** and **30**. It's generally easier and richer to mine older memories that have bedded in, though both of the above examples flout this rule for compelling reasons.

Mining memories

If you want to embrace **Write what you know** the obvious starting point is autobiography.

- Write your life story or fragments of it and choose details to explore through fictional work. You might also pursue memoir, a tricky form that requires great self-awareness and compassion. How did the world shape you?[2]
- Start every day with writing 'I remember when/where/how/why...' and see what follows as the memories start to surface.
- Keep a book of dreams or any other kind of diary that appeals to you. Try writing early or late when your mind is most relaxed.
- Keep an observational 'book of life' as glimpsed through your eyes. Can be jottings or reflective. Capture places, characters, events, conversations, phrases as they happen in order to expand what you know.

Sita Brahmachari started writing her first book, *Artichoke Hearts* (winner of the 2011 Waterstone's Children's Book Prize), just after her mother-in-law died. Her children had accompanied her on visits to the hospice and originally the story was written for them, to commemorate their grandmother. However, Sita's way in to the story was through her imagination.

> 'The invention of the artichoke heart charm that the dying Nana Josie gives to her granddaughter Mira on her twelfth birthday was my way into writing a book about love and loss and inheritance. I knew the subject

of my book before I set out. It came from the heart. I wanted to write a novel that explored how deeply young people can feel the great operatic moments of life that an understanding of the process of death and birth offer. To deny young people these experiences seemed to me to be limiting their emotional landscape. All this I knew I wanted to explore when I set out to write *Artichoke Hearts*, but I found I needed a symbol, a metaphor to carry me through the work. It was only when I plucked from my imagination the artichoke heart charm that the story, exploring the many layers of a twelve-year-old girl's tender heart, began to emerge:

> "I've given you this [charm], Mira, because you're so special to me…how can I explain? Most people, by the time they get old, have grown themselves tough little shells around their hearts. Babies like little Laila, start off with tender, loving trusting hearts, but gradually, gradually they learn to protect themselves and, as the years go by, grow tougher and tougher layers. Look at this! The outside layers of an artichoke are so tough they're not even worth eating, but they get more and more tender as you come closer to the heart." ' (*Artichoke Hearts*, p.38)

Perhaps in writing you never truly get beyond your own childhood. As Sita says, 'We all remember the rites of passage moments, and the times when, like it or not, we found that we had to wrap a protective layer around our hearts.'

Who needs what you know?

Real is a marketing tool and true-life experience sometimes deemed more important than whether someone can beautifully bring to life an imagined world. In our celebrity-obsessed culture, fame or infamy is the fastest route to getting published or produced.

The 'authentic experience' that is fashionable is often what the dominant culture wants to learn about or incorporate. You might not feel comfortable being put in the position of educator or representative about an aspect of your identity or life story. You may not want to comply with other people's expectations of you in terms of subject matter.

At worst, writers can be pushed into a niche decided for them. By favouring lived experience over imagination, knowledge over sensibility, the rule **Write what you know** has also been used to exclude people from writing outside of their age, culture, class, gender, time or circumstances. In theatre I have seen this promote a segregation of the imagination. Two ridiculous true-life examples are of a white writer being berated by a senior theatre critic for writing a 'black play' and a black writer being asked by a white director 'What d'you want to write so many white characters for?'

Here's another example. What's your view? Was the Royal Court Theatre being patronising and inauthentic in setting up a Young Muslim Writers Group or was it helping to bring into the spotlight stories untold within a wider constituency? Why should these young writers be given special support by virtue of their religion or culture? Why are they being encouraged to write from a 'Muslim position' or about 'Muslim life' in order to access their share of public funding? Should they be so incentivised to **Write what you know**?

Write what you know emotionally

In one sense, of course, all fictional work is autobiography. Novelist Chris Paling, recently acclaimed for *Nimrod's Shadow* (2010), says:

> 'It wasn't until I'd been writing a while that I realised I'd misinterpreted the rule 'Write what you know'. What it actually means is to write what you know emotionally. Look at your own processes and apply them, or versions of them, to your characters. This will give them a more

useful authenticity. Once I applied this I found it much easier to bring my characters to life.'

An actor approaches character in a similar way. Through feeling rather than knowing; empathy rather than biography. How else could an actor play Medea or Macbeth or a writer create such characters? What you know of life is not irrelevant, but it is the sensitivity with which you process your experience, rather than the experience itself that you draw on.

Screenwriter Terry Hodgkinson says,

> 'Be very careful when writing about emotions which you have never experienced or witnessed yourself. If you get it wrong the audience will spot it a mile off.'

We've all read or seen work with false notes, but is that to do with lack of knowledge or lack of imagination?

Beware of personal obsessions

Everyone has hobby horses. Whilst these may provide authentic detail when relevant to the story, your personal obsessions won't necessarily interest others to the same extent. Consider how sparingly to use what you know.

Write what you don't know

Multi-award-winning playwright Bryony Lavery loves the challenge of writing about unfamiliar subjects. I recently saw *Kursk* (2009), her immersive theatrical experience set inside the doomed Russian submarine. The piece explored an emotionally repressed male world, alien to most in the audience. It was a world that couldn't be further from Bryony's open-heartedness.

> 'Write what you know. I never do, which is why now I know a lot about submarines, boxing, paedophilia, murder, Alzheimer's, bombs, Hadron physics, Chinese tombs, war, I could go on.'

This link between creativity and learning is at the heart of many writing processes. It also defines certain genres – the historical novel being an obvious example. Gaps in expertise are filled by research (**Rule 5**) and in drama the collaboration between writer, director and actors often fills personal, experiential gaps. Through exploring and piecing our perspectives together, we find an emotional truth. Discovering worlds beyond yourself enables you to grow, to gain wisdom. It offers an exciting and expansive creative journey.

Make it up

Writing always draws on what you know and what you don't know yet. It's about being in a state of unknowing, however you personally express that feeling; in the zone, in flow, in a waking dream. On this creative journey you draw on everything known and unknown. Writing is about being as honest to what's in your heart as you can be and as free to imagine the opposite.

The obvious and beautiful truth about writing is that you make it up as you go along. No land is out of reach to you, no world impossible.

RULE BREAKER 1

Write to discover what you don't know yet

RULE 2

Find your authentic voice

Authentic voice is what we're all searching for as readers or writers. It feels like a fundamental principle of writing. As a concept it's fraught with contradiction, not least in terms of context and notions of meaning. This discussion will focus on the practicalities from a writer's point of view.

Your voice is that unique aspect of your writing that sets it apart; the originality that everyone talks about, what commissioners are looking for. It is as complex and distinct as you are, expressing your deepest self – your instinct, sensibility, world view, unique relationship with language, rhythm, character and story. When you write, your whole being meets the material you're communicating.

As screenwriter Chris Lunt puts it:

> 'It's like a piece of music – forget rules and convention, I don't know them and have never consciously adhered to them – what you ideally want is for someone to pick up your script, start reading, and without looking at the front page, know it's by you.'

Finding your authentic voice as a writer is almost always about removing the blocks to facing yourself, getting out of your own way. These blocks may be a lack of confidence; a fear of others seeing the 'real' you; of wanting your work to be perfect or of over analyzing. Sometimes I read a very self-aware and polished piece, but the soul, the authentic voice is missing. Interestingly, this voice feels most evident in the gaps or the rawer moments, even as they betray the underlying weakness of the work. Anyone who commissions writers will tell you the same thing. Craft can be worked on. The voice needs to sing.

This is because when we engage with a writer's work, we search for a truth. Not a conclusive or absolute truth, but an ever-changing, contradictory, moment to moment truth. How true is their world to my world, how honest to itself? What is this writer saying and what does that reveal to me about myself? Your honesty and creative freedom as a writer, combined with your skill, invites your reader to experience a world that they couldn't possibly imagine without you.

Most writers seem to have developed their unique perspective on the world through a sense of being an outsider in some way. This might have been compounded by some wrench in early life, such as being a first-generation migrant or experiencing a difficult family situation. You feel compelled to express yourself through writing to connect with the world. Your struggle and growth lives on in the personality and energy of your voice.

Screenwriter Stephen Brady articulates this as an inner breach. I hesitate to suggest that it's universal, but it does make sense of my own experience and that of many writers I have worked with.

> 'The desire to write comes from a place of unhappiness. With writing as with any form of creativity you're trying to make sense of the mysteries of life, you're trying to make things whole. At some stage the childhood idyll is shattered. How and when that happens is crucial. As is the support and love you get – or don't get – from those around you. For some that breach is repaired and life goes on. For others it's never repaired. They become writers doomed to endlessly attempt to make things whole – a job that never gets any easier because the task is impossible.'

I've often observed how this writerly sense of incompletion, of trying to achieve some kind of closure, translates into the story of the main character's unconscious need – the wound that needs to be healed, the shadow self. I discuss this concept fully in **Rule 14.**

Can an original voice be learned or lost?

I don't think an authentic voice needs to be learned because we all have one, however buried or bizarre. I think that once you have rooted your voice, you can strengthen and develop it through practice. Trust your inner truth and be brave enough to stand up for it.

The paradox is that you can never hear your own voice the way it sounds to others and therefore, the less self-conscious you are about your voice, the stronger it will be. You need to trust yourself and your world view so you're not fretting about what you should say, or even in the first draft how to say it.

A genre voice can be learned. For example, you might develop an *EastEnders* voice when you write for that soap. Sometimes there's a terrible struggle when a writer uses their distinctive authentic voice to express inauthentic material. This has happened occasionally to friends of mine who have moved into TV from theatre, getting their first jobs on soaps. Theatre demands a very forceful voice, a big personality. In collaborative TV shows you must partially submerge your uniqueness within the identity of the already established series/serial. Some writers love this process, others feel hampered by it.

An original writer's voice can also lose its power or identity. This may stem from an inability to chime with the time, a lack of inner growth, fresh material or a host of other reasons. The voice seems somehow unrooted and we don't trust it anymore. For example, many of the greatest writers retell a version of the same core story for years and the source material of their childhood can serve a lifetime of writing. However, a cultural shift, a new trend, can unexpectedly call into question the repetition of character types, themes or images across a writer's oeuvre. Voice is always dependent upon context, your acuity in relation to the changing world.

Discover your personal subtext

You can play to the strength of your personal subtext by matching your voice to material and medium. In art as in life, the harder you strive, the more it eludes you. You can only be more yourself by *being* yourself – flawed, weird, wonderful you.

I run a workshop called *Discover your personal subtext,* in which we use exercises to trick your psyche. Being guided through such practice can help new writers bypass the conscious self and, as Jung described it, embrace the shadow self. Such exercises are about your deepest need to communicate and the results are often revelatory. A writer may realize that what they really want to write is not what they are writing, but rather what they thought they definitely *didn't* want to write. How often in life as in fiction, doing what you don't want is the path to finding what you do.

This book is not a workshop substitute – it's hard to play tricks on yourself. Still, you can follow the tips below without any guidance. They are worth trying, particularly for those intellectuals or neurotics among you who love to over-analyse. Free your imagination.

- Automatic writing in all its guises can release your authentic voice and also help you write through blocks. Try to write against the clock, if only for ten minutes. Don't lift your pen from the paper, gibberish is fine. Never stop to read over what you've written. Don't edit. This discipline enables freedom. When you do read it back you'll be amazed at your creativity.
- For many, the best time to write is first thing in the morning. Being in that dream state helps. You can trick yourself by resetting the alarm and drifting back to sleep. Try writing down your dreams as soon as you wake or write down anything else that enters your mind. In writing it down, all that you're doing is affirming the relationship between the chaotic playground of your unconscious and your pen. If

you do it every day, you'll find that your writing becomes more fluent and free.

- Always keep a notebook with you for those little nonsense snippets of voices that enter your head, or for tiny sensory observations or feelings, as mentioned in **Rule 1**. They say that we only retain such details for three minutes. The good stuff will surely resurface in another form, but jotting can be a vital prompt. This notebook will further your present project but you may also develop left-field random fragments into new characters. The simple act of keeping the notebook develops your awareness, your powers of observation and discrimination.

- You can use anything to prompt an automatic writing exercise. Take thirty cards/bits of paper. Choose ten places, ten characters and ten obstacles. Write a few words to describe them or draw them. Put them into three piles so that you choose a place, a character and an obstacle from each. Randomly you might end up with fur coat woman on a hillside with the obstacle of a crying child or a demon spinning through the kitchen with the obstacle of a wedding ring. Spend ten minutes automatic writing against the clock to create a story. Again don't let the pen leave the paper, don't edit. The funny thing is that it doesn't really matter what the cards say or what the prompt is. Your personal subtext will blaze through.

- Spend an afternoon playing with children or adults or both, making up imaginary games and stories. Children are endlessly inventive and inspire creativity. If you don't know any kids, get to know some actors. Actors can play and they nurture their inner child. Join an improvisation class and write after the session.

- Is there a creative space you share with others where you do feel in touch with your authentic self, where you lose all sense of time and space and just free flow? Expand your boundaries there. If you feel free in painting, love-making, dancing, cooking or making music, let your imagination run wilder there. Taking risks in life can boost your confidence and creativity in writing too. Creativity is all about embracing risk. If you continually push your own boundaries, you become more true to yourself.

What's at stake for you?

What have you gained through writing? Why do you write? What's the biggest risk you've ever taken in your writing? What have you risked losing or what have you lost in order to write? Was it really a risk for you? What means most to you in the world? Would you risk that for your writing? What else would you risk then? Is it enough or too much?

Authenticity is about courage

Taking risks is about shedding your own façade. We understand this when we're writing characters but it's harder to recognise in ourselves. So think of yourself for a moment as the character at the heart of your own story, the story of you going out to confront the world as a writer. What are you taking from the world for your writing? What are you giving back? Has the world responded in the way you expected? Was it better or worse? How have you been obstructed? Who has supported you on your writing journey so far professionally, emotionally, financially? What's the worst thing someone could say to you on your writing journey?

- Draw yourself a little timeline for your story *My Life as a Writer,* or make up a title. Put on the high and low turning points, so that you have a series of up and down spikes across a central timeline. Imagine how your story might turn out for the very best – create a happy resolution to your timeline beyond today's date. Make it as far in the future as feels realistic. Reflect on the journey that will take you from here to there.

Is authentic voice a principle for writers?

There are many areas of experimental writing that relish intertextuality, authorlessness or collectivity. I think an authentic voice still emerges through the point of view of a group of writers or the personal narrative of the audience-reader. What can seem to one person a false, self-conscious voice can seem to another an acute comment on the fakery and narcissism of modern life. This is why the notion of authentic voice, so meaningful for us as writers, can seem banal when placed in a wider cultural context or subjected to academic scrutiny.

Though as writers we are committed to catching the truth of a moment, when we re-read what we've written, our feeling about that truth often changes too (**Rule 32**). In another context, the truth a writer settles for can become its opposite for the audience-reader.

To take an obvious example, many works that we consider great were once denigrated. The Georgians banned *King Lear* because they had a mad king and the Victorians preferred the play with a happy ending. I think we all recognise this kind of political cowardice. *Saved* (1965) by Edward Bond, *Blasted* (1995) by Sarah Kane and *Mercury Fur* (2005) by Philip Ridley are all plays that were vilified on a first outing. How many disturbing works of brilliance never make it to the public realm at all? Are they less or more authentic for being feared by the dominant culture of the time?

Having an authentic voice, whatever that means to you, is no sure-fire route to success. But what is the point in writing at all unless you are as true to yourself as you can be and take pride or pleasure in your writing life. On the other hand, if the meaning that a reader-audience brings to your work differs from your own, in what sense can we talk about an authentic voice?

OK, so we're only on **Rule 2** but I'm going to stand up for this principle of authenticity. Meaning may be fluid, but integrity to a moment feels specific when you write and when you read. Writers are a conduit for honest expression of self and vision. At their best, in a moment of complete connection, they express this authenticity on the page. Surely this is why great work can live on, communicating a truth across culture, history and time, regardless of whether this truth was intended.

Still, a writer is also a magician who weaves a spell. What we see as authentic may simply be a mirage, the height of artifice, a construction of supposed truth that *we* place on the creative process, partly because the writer was so damn deft.

RULE BREAKER 2

Be true to the moment – nothing is fixed

RULE 3

Start with a strong premise and a compelling pitch

And if these incidents now seem full of significance and all of a piece, it's probably because I'm looking at them in the light of what came later...

Kazuo Ishiguro, *Never Let Me Go*

The term 'premise' can be misleading for writers, not least the idea of starting with one. I don't want to confuse you further, but the notion of premise can be interpreted in subtly different ways. Lajos Egri and John Truby represent two trends.

Egri, in *The Art of Dramatic Writing* (1946), uses premise to sum up the world view that is argued out through the action of a story. A premise is the 'motivating force' that drives a conflict of values. Your story plays out from, towards and through the premise, dialectically turning over its central thesis, proving it, then disproving it or staring at it sideways from a new point of view. In Egri's notion of premise, the writer clearly takes sides.

For John Truby in *The Anatomy of Story* (2007) and for many in the film industry, a premise is simply 'your story stated in one sentence.' It is your persuasive pitch. And though it implicitly contains the message that Egri describes, the moral of the tale is more hidden and the movement of the story more explicit and concrete. Truby might describe Egri's description of premise as 'theme'.

So how does this difference play out in practice and does it matter? Take a look for yourself. I've used famous works from each medium that you have almost certainly read or seen. The first version emphasises a moral approach, the second storytelling. Note that both approaches offer a premise that is inherently ironic, containing the potential for argument. After all, without contradiction and conflict, there can be no meaningful change.

Value premise

All are equal but some are more equal than others (*Animal Farm*).

Love conquers everything, even death (*Romeo and Juliet*).

You don't need to go in search of success – it resides in you (*It's a Wonderful Life*).

Story premise

The animals overthrow the farmer to reorganise the farm on an equal basis, but they reckoned without the pigs (*Animal Farm*).

Two teenagers fall in love against their families wishes. They rebel against their fathers and face death rather than be parted (*Romeo and Juliet*).

A man who has failed to leave his small-town life is about to commit suicide when an angel shows him what his town would be like if he had never lived there (*It's a Wonderful Life*).

Clearly premise is not simply an imaginative starting point. It describes what happens to your characters as a *result* of the story. It is the foregone conclusion of an argument between two or more positions – the summary of the winning argument as much as a proposition for an argument. This is why many writers insist that you have to know the end of your story at the beginning.

Other writers take issue with this. They are more comfortable pitching a value premise – a world view and an approach, rather than the worked out story that proves their thesis. Philip

Ridley, for example, always talks about his early ideas in terms of atmosphere, values, theme and characters. His play *Leaves of Glass* (2007) changed entirely between our first conversation and the first draft. This was partly because I took over Soho Theatre and the space there implied a different kind of play, but it also reflected Phil's process as a writer. 'I don't know where I'm going with a story,' he explains. 'That's the best way to end up at the right place.'

Pros and cons

So as a writer, what are the advantages of knowing your premise upfront? Well, it can help you shape and focus your work as defined by the outposts of an argument. Some say that finding a unique premise is the basis for all storytelling.

Certainly, without a premise, it can be tough to develop a clear and compelling pitch. Some dramatists believe that a story exists in the air between people rather than as words on the page. Tanika Gupta shares her thoughts on this:

> 'Often ideas haunt me for a long time before I can work out how to tell the story. Sometimes, it can be as big and vague as 'I want to write a story about the history of Asians in Victorian Britain' (my play for the RSC) or as specific as 'I want to write about friendship between two young men' (*White Boy*, 2007/8, NYT/Soho). The more you pitch your story, or the more you tell your story – the clearer it becomes in your head. Verbalising an idea often helps me to be clearer before, during and after I write it. Ultimately I guess, if you as the writer don't know how to explain your story, the resulting script will be unclear as well and you'll have a heck of a time trying to get directors and actors to unpick your words.'

When you discuss your work with others, their response may also feed your imagination. However, some writers experience the opposite – that you lose your hold on an emerging story by sharing it too soon, you dissipate the energy. I've worked with writers who are fiercely protective of their inner process. I empathise with this. It may depend on whether you're by nature introverted or extroverted, whether you need to be alone to gain clarity or prefer to work out your ideas with others. This can simply be a question of timing. I remember finding it hard to verbally pitch my walkabout play *Hoxton Story* (2005) before I had written it. I couldn't get beyond saying something flat and lifeless like 'a site-specific piece that exposes the negative impact of regeneration.' This told people nothing about the rich experience they would have. My mind was just whirling with characters, images, flickers of story and possible encounters for the audience but I could only have created a false coherence. Eventually I started sharing these moments and metaphors and I learnt that with the right collaborators, this was enough.

If you're going to a meeting to talk about your work, you would be wise to try out your ideas on a friend beforehand. I've been on the receiving end of shallow, ubiquitous pitches and they're generally a waste of time. You really do need some feeling, image, character or scenario that you can talk about with passion or clarity. Or work with a trusted collaborator who loves your writing and understands your approach. Writing may be all about accepting your own failure, but you can scupper a potentially beautiful project by offering it up for interrogation before it's able to defend itself.

Some writers are great verbal storytellers and some great writers are not. In my experience, being good at selling an idea does not necessarily relate to a writer's talent. When high concept was in fashion a few years back, I remember talking to some student screenwriters who spoke as if their ideas were the work itself. Indeed many were so high concept that the premise negated any need for a screenplay to be written at all!

Multi-plot stories and complex character portraits are notoriously hard to turn into simple pitches, especially when the meaning comes from well observed relationships rather than an idea.

However, internal character transformation is the meat of great storytelling, as all actors know. Who needs a high concept hook when you've got Jude Law?

In some commissioning contexts, the premise has been determined for you. For example, on a TV series or an issue-led theatre project, you might write to a brief, within someone else's moral framework.

If you have to pitch, here are some tips...

- Ensure you've come up with an original idea. You can strengthen it by doing a 'What if...? riff' around your premise i.e. free associating questions. You may want to use why...? what...? and how...? questions as well as what if...?
- To kick-start a one-liner try this formula: (flawed) main character wants (specific goal) but (antagonist inner and/ or outer) is in her way. When she is compelled (to do something new) she has a chance to (act and grow) or risk (whatever is at stake). See what you've got and develop it from there.
- A simpler version is to just answer what happened to whom and what did they do about it? Show that your main character is in action/conflict and that the stakes of succeeding/failing are high for them and us.
- Imply the whole story, usually through the set-up's promise of an ironic twist, but don't worry about giving the end unless it's your trump card and/or you're begged for it. Treat your pitch as temptation. Create one or more key questions in the mind of your potential commissioner.
- Try to convey in a few words the vision of the world that the audience-reader will encounter. This might be about the perspective it's being told from, the tone, the visual style, the language, the sensory and emotional feel of it.

Through this, you can imply a sense of who your story is for.

- In addition to your story pitch, it can be helpful to indicate a sense of scale, so that your potential commissioner can guesstimate budget parameters. In theatre, cast size can make or break; in publishing, wordage is key; in film, the location, action, casting and special effects. Don't get bogged down in this, just be aware.

Premises, Premises.

The danger of a rigid premise is that you create a didactic story. However, no premise can stifle your imagination if you're open and flexible. After all, the same premise could generate thousands of different stories. There is no betrayal in changing your mind. What emerges from your unconscious during the writing process might totally contradict what you thought you wanted to say at the beginning. That's OK. A premise exists to support your imaginative journey, not vice versa.

Some writers like to have their premise in view as they write, above the screen or on the wall. They argue that without it, they would waste precious writing time following tangents and instincts, then end up having to scrap most of it. Other writers are happier working creatively with some compelling 'what ifs.' A few writers leave it up to the reader-audience to decide what their work means and they refuse to ever define or discuss it.

If you are someone who writes well organically, then you may have to write first and sell after, or build trust in your process over time through key relationships. You need to be commissioned for your brilliant writing rather than your dazzling pitch.

RULE BREAKER 3

Let the meaning find you

RULE 4

Read what you want to write

It is what you read when you don't have to that determines what you will be when you can't help it.

Oscar Wilde

Read what you want to write is one of those pieces of advice that is entirely personal to your process. It's worth a short discussion because it is so often said.

Make a list of your favourite works in any medium and then look for common ground between them and your project. What do you notice? You probably read the kind of work that haunts your own, that has already found its way into your writerly DNA. If your favourite works have no connection at all to what you're writing, then you might want to question whether you're writing the kind of story that will fulfill you most.

Common sense tells you to read what's out there in the same vein as your project, if only to avoid duplicating what already exists. At the very least you'll want to ensure that your angle is unique. You might also want to immerse yourself in a particular genre or style as a preparation for writing. Be an active, critical reader or audience. Ask yourself how a writer achieves their result, why it works and what you can learn from that.

What's lacking in your work?

On a more subtle level, you can read for what's lacking in your own work, or in a given passage or scene. Try looking at a play or novel that excels in this quality. If your writing lacks levity read comedy; if it's cliché ridden, read a wordsmith; if the narrative is stalling, read a great storyteller. This isn't about copying another person's style or saying 'I wish I wrote more like J.G. Ballard.' Rather, it's to examine how you can model an aspect of someone else's brilliant technique, in order to write more like yourself.

Bend or Break the rule

The danger of **Read what you want to write** for new writers is that it may compound a problem. Consciously or unconsciously most of us start out emulating our favourite writers. If someone points this out to you, don't be too tempted to take it as a compliment! If imitation is an issue for you, try reading anything *except* the kind of stuff you're writing, at least during the writing process. Include work from outside your medium as well as beyond your niche. This can help you develop a more distinct voice.

RULE BREAKER 4

Write what you want to read

RULE 5

You can't do too much research

Research is important. You care deeply about the real world you're using as source material and you want to share your discoveries in writing. But something is wrong. You did all this research to avoid sounding like a tourist and now you're sounding like a tour guide instead.

Too much research in a piece of writing feels literal rather than transcendent. Strangely, for all those painstaking details, it feels fake and increases the sense that the writer is an outsider on the world of their story. The work feels bogged down in exposition, in giving proofs. Though at times this may add colour and truthful detail, it can also hinder the dramatic movement of your fictional world.

When the research screams 'I'm important!' it expresses insecurity. Letting go can be a challenge for serious writers, particularly when researching a significant material reality. Usually this is to do with your deep immersion in the world of your research. Sometimes, an overwhelming sense of responsibility or a fear of being inauthentic stops you feeling free to develop your story or certain characters in it. This is a particular challenge when your work is based on people who are alive and there may be emotional, political, cultural or legal issues around their representation. Sometimes you're intent on proving to yourself or your reader-audience that you truly know this world.

In your heart you may feel that the real world of your research is more alive to you than the work emerging in your imagination. Or you may be dismayed by the conflict between the fictional and the real. If either of these situations sounds familiar and you're in the midst of research, then try writing something completely different that is entirely fictional. Reconnect with your free, imaginative self.

Make it your own

- Put complete distance between yourself and the research and start to live fully in your imagined world. Trust that your imagination will use what's needed and discard what isn't. You can always check facts or details at a later stage. Sometimes it helps, as an exercise, to explore the trap that you fear falling into, the approach that feels wrong and irresponsible. Writing out your worst nightmare can free you up to move beyond it.

- When living people are your resource, always be very clear about what you are doing and why. Be straightforward about the boundaries when you ask for their involvement in a project. Take responsibility and then you can relax about it. They need to sign a contract giving you legal permission to use their story or you need to be clear that it will not be identifiable but is just a springboard for fiction. Or perhaps you want to use their 'disapproval' within the work itself, as Alexander Masters does in *The Genius in My Basement* (2011). You can each decide what terms feel comfortable, but it's vital to have clarity before you start talking.

- In redrafting, edit out any details which don't enhance the story. Be a true insider on the world you're writing about. You are the expert. Take it for granted.

- Next time, try approaching research strictly on a need to know basis. You'll be surprised how much research can be done on the hoof, particularly through the internet. Of course this depends on your topic. The more informed you are, the more probing your questions will be. Equally, naivety has the advantage of taking nothing for granted.

- Chunk the research – do it a segment at a time. So if you don't reach Cambodia until the second half of your novel and it has no bearing on the first half, deal with it later.
- For further issues around authenticity, representation and offence see **Rules 29** and **30**.

Research as creative preparation

Overfamiliarity can be as much of an issue as lack of research. Photographing a world you know well is one way to help you see it afresh. All writers have a creative research process, which may be simply about daydreaming and trying out different imaginative scenarios. Philip Ridley explains his unique preparation.

> 'Photography has always been a big part of how I develop my written works. I've been taking photographs since I was about fifteen. I always walk around with a camera on me. I use the camera like a kind of sketch book. I take photos of anything that catches my eye. There's no direction or plan to it; the texture of some brickwork, a crowd of people, an interesting cloud (oh, I've got lots of photos of clouds), someone who's dressed in a certain way. I photograph it all. My main two subjects though are the East End of London and my friends, and both of these strands impact on the writing in a very direct way. It's very important for me that I have a very specific setting for the play. I have to know the setting this well because my writing is, in many ways, a sort of heightened reality. When I'm focusing in on a play, I work with friends to create a very strong photographic image of what I think the characters might look like. Luckily, most of my friends now tend to be actors so they are really able to improvise with me. And then I start to pin all these photos up on the walls around the desk where I write. I write in a small back room. The windows are blacked out so I have no distractions. I look at the photos of locations and characters and...the world of the play starts to become totally alive for me. I hope.'

These photographs are works of art in themselves and we exhibited some of them outside the auditorium where the plays we did together were performed. They were also a kind of mood preparation for the audience.

In my experience...

One of my first theatre jobs was as a researcher for a playwright at Theatre Royal Stratford East back in 1988. This involved me finding and interviewing older East End working-class women in their homes (mostly first-generation migrants) and recording their life stories. It was a wonderful process, but for me there were a lot of issues concerning the fictionalisation of these women. The playwright's characters were composites but the true details of the women's lives were used in the play, leading to some confusion for the women who came to see it. Today I suspect it would have been done as verbatim drama.

When I wrote and directed *Hoxton Story* in 2005, a site-specific walkabout performance, there was a short verbatim introduction to the piece in the theatre, before we moved out onto the real streets and into a fictional world. The whole piece was informed by forty hours of interviews about change with Hoxton residents, mainly from the housing estates in the area. We catalogued these as an oral history archive (deposited with Hackney Libraries for perpetuity). I also edited a booklet containing these interviews and Leo Asemota's portrait photographs of residents and we set up an interactive website. Because the site-specific fiction took place in the real world of my research, it enabled me to honour and interrogate both processes fully. I had my own passionate perspective as an artist about people's stories and what I had experienced in the area. I could play freely with the blurring of boundaries between reality and fiction and literally leave my research behind.

RULE BREAKER 5

Leave the research behind

RULE 6

Write an outline before you write

An outline can mean anything from the bare bones of a story, (a few lines, as Aristotle suggests), to a one page synopsis, a full treatment or a step outline/beat sheet that details every scene and unit of action. An outline can be for yourself, for a pitch, or as a stage in the commissioning process. Short or long, brief or detailed, it is the map of your story.

Some of you take pleasure in creating order out of chaos, of honing the story at an early stage, of knowing the destination of the luggage in the hall.[3] If you are the kind of writer who works outside-in, plot before character, consciously constructing a world first and emotionally deepening it later, this process of mapping it out may instinctively work for you. You'll enjoy a sense of freedom and feel less daunted by the act of writing. Knowing your direction can help you set up the next part of the story and you may feel that this saves time at the rewrite stage. For certain genres that require intricate plotting (e.g. crime), an outline may be particularly helpful. Many novelists need to feel a sense of the whole before they can make an investment in the long haul.

In film and TV, great emphasis is placed on getting the outline right. A screenplay is more structured than a play and the financial stakes are often higher. There are many successful writers who have trained themselves to work in this way. Novelists and playwrights may also create outlines for submission to agents, theatres and publishing houses, enabling front line readers to assess the story potential. Gone are those heady days of free commissions in theatre when you could write what you like. Now there is a whole layer of bureaucracy – artistic directors, literary managers, executives, boards, marketing, casting, funders – all wanting to know what they're going to get before it arrives, pretty much guaranteeing that nothing surprising will arrive at all.

Many new writers instinctively prefer a more organic, spontaneous process. In-Sook Chappell's debut play *This Isn't Romance* won the Verity Bargate Award 2007. I helped her develop it from her first draft, directed it at Soho Theatre and for Radio 3. The theatre wanted a detailed outline of her next play before commissioning it, so she's been trying out a new process.

> 'It took me a long time to be able to say I was a writer. I only really felt confident after winning the VBA and having my play produced. If you had asked me what my first couple of plays were about I wouldn't have been able to tell you. I would start writing and hope that my subconscious kicked in and something interesting would happen. This is great if you are happy never working on commission. I think being able to make a living from writing is making the transition between writing for yourself and hoping it will eventually be produced (while temping/waitressing/ other) to being able to explain what it is you are trying to do and convince people to commission your work. I think this is about balancing the internal and the external or being clear about structure and story. At the moment I am working from the outside in, as opposed to the inside out. I am starting with what the play is about, the structure and the story and then trying to get deep inside the character, make it really personal, as opposed to the story coming from my subconscious.'

I have heard the same experience articulated in different ways by many writers at this breakthrough stage. Only through experimenting on your own terms will you discover the process that works best for you.

Why the plan?

Gatekeeper rules around precision planning are rarely about writing. They are about marketing or financial risk mitigation, the risk lying with your unruly writer's imagination. These rules may be there to help the producers sleep at night, but for many of you they are a nightmare, the equivalent of talking about a dream you haven't had yet. An organic approach is the rule-breaker here but it may mean not writing for TV much unless there is a revolution in the industry. I encourage you to start one of course!

Accepting the treatment – how do I do it?

Expanding on the premise (**Rule 3**), the feel of the outline is expected to reflect the style, tone and visual world of your story as well as its use of suspense and language. In other words, it should give us a taste of how exciting and brilliantly written your story will be and raise questions in the same way that the story will. Your outline should take the reader to the end of the story.

- Where and when is it set? Who are the key characters? What are their goals? What is the conflict, and the stakes? What happens?
- If you know the overarching story premise, chunk it into key scenes or events. Use sections or chapter breaks and title or number them if that helps. Start to fill the gaps between those major events. Then break down each scene into beats. Just keep chunking down as far as it feels useful.
- If you don't know the big picture then chunk it up from key moments into scenarios/scenes/sections until you have connected them up into a whole. See Roy Williams' approach (p.52).

Companies and individuals in TV and film usually have their own preference as to length and style of outlines – check before you put in the work. For theatres it tends to be looser and the individuality of your approach is more respected. Literary agents and publishers vary hugely so check individual guidelines.

Refusing the treatment

I've rarely met a writer who enjoyed writing outlines for commissioners (rough notes for yourself is a different matter). As soon as your characters start talking to each other, everything changes, so what's the point? On the other hand, writers are generally happy to present their ideas in a way that works for them and doesn't waste precious time.

BAFTA-winning screenwriter of *Control* and *Nowhere Boy*, Matt Greenhalgh, suggests that you need the confidence to bend the rules and suit your own needs when preparing outlines for producers.

> 'The convention I personally railed against was that of the flowery prose treatment for a movie or TV idea. I would spend weeks writing an intricate book about what I wanted to write in the script, exhausting myself, poring over every word, trying to make it thrilling and compelling. I couldn't let go as I was a novelist in my head first before this movie-thing. Then I'd get upset when notes were sent back and people didn't 'get it'. And for what? This wasn't where my energy should be sapped. Like a boxer punching himself out before the first bell. This was the normal practice before writing the screenplay i.e. the actual thing that *mattered*. So I stopped torturing myself. I refused to do detailed paragraphs and told that to producers upfront. Instead I would use precise bullet points when outlining the story. Simple, straightforward.'

In general, people start writing because they feel they must. Some have a sense of the whole, some don't. If you start before you're ready, you may have to stop and start again and be endlessly re-drafting. However, readiness has nothing to do with knowing exactly what you are going to write. Writing is improvising and only you know when you are ready to play and what rules you need in place before you start.

Your plan will rarely translate directly into your script because writing doesn't work like that. Luckily there is a wonderful paradox. The more you try to control your imagination, the less original its fruits will be. Those producers need your unique voice. They want you to free your imagination but they can't help you get there and some of what they ask for may get in your way. They are talking to you from the institutional point of view (they would say the audience's), rather than enabling your individual artistic process.

The many rules around conscious planning – from industry demands to prescriptive guru guides – can be confusing and incapacitating for new writers. Once fear and judgement creep in, your instinctive voice starts to fade. You can waste six months trying to get the plan right and then lose interest in the project or even decide that you're no good as a writer. If this is you, listen to your own truth and please just throw away whatever rule book you're following and get back to doing what you love – writing. Writing is the process of discovering what you don't know rather than the presentation of what you do.

Dennis Kelly, writer of hit musical *Matilda*, also refuses the treatment. In theatre, as an acclaimed playwright, he can simply say no. In TV, where he is best known for the series *Pulling*, he acknowledges that the collaborative aspects of series/serials may necessitate outlines. However, in film, he and his agent have found a brilliant way around the treatment issue which I think is worth sharing in full.

> 'My feeling on treatments or pitches is that if they are not how you work as a writer then doing them is a betrayal of the thing you're writing. Personally I find that if I write a treatment or pitch I will probably do a worse job on the script itself – I have no idea how a character should behave until I've heard them speak, so a treatment will force me to make decisions based on information I don't really have, essentially dishonest decisions. But I have also found

that if you politely explain this to most film producers or directors they are actually quite sympathetic. In my view, a first draft of a film is really an offer, a sometimes clumsy mess of ideas and thoughts that is sort of saying 'what about this?' You get some things right, you get some things wrong, some things open avenues to be explored, some things need to be discarded. But if you can put that down in the form of a script rather than a treatment you can probably get a lot more eloquent about what you feel the thing should look like in the end.

The reason producers would not want you to go to first draft straight away without knowing the detail of what you're up to is that contractually the first draft is actually quite expensive, so it's understandable that they would be nervous. My agent has very cleverly come up with a way to get over this hurdle by offering to do a cheaper first draft, somewhere between the cost of doing a treatment and what the first draft would be, a sort of pre-first draft (which actually always ends up being the first draft), with the full fees being made up further down the line, like when you deliver, for example. This allays the nerves of the producer and shows them you are serious about what you say; that essentially your first draft is really a treatment in the form of a script, not just a way for you to avoid hard work and get cash quickly.

I also offer to have as many conversations about the script and ideas before as they'd like, as conversations are general things and can be useful in identifying the problem issues you may face in the script without handcuffing you in the way that documents do. It should be said that this approach should only be used if you're willing to walk away – if you say to some producers that you won't write a treatment they are well within their rights to say 'fine, forget it, we'll get someone else.' And of course if you want to write a treatment or you think in this particular case it will help then it's fine. But if you don't or it won't then you really do need to find a way to protect your process.'

This seems an excellent model. Many writers achieve more by getting lost in the flow of the writing process than struggling with their plan. If you love risk and a feeling of freedom and dreaming while awake, you probably don't definitively plan and even writing sequentially may not work for you. Some of you write key scenes as they occur and find links in original, unplanned ways to structure a whole.

Other plans

Writing outlines is not the only way to plan. Many writers instinctively make use of mind-mapping techniques to connect their ideas, which can start from any point.[4] Roy Williams describes his process:

> 'Knowing what to write about is dead easy. All I have to do is read a paper, see what is going on in the world, or I can draw from the well of my own experiences. Knowing *who* I am writing about is what gives me sleepless nights. I love imagery, I cannot write a word without an image in my head. I draw a circle with a dot in the centre, which represents my image which can be a person, object etc. I then write outwards from that dot, shaping and reshaping as I go, that is the blueprint for my play.'

Daydreaming and mulling over ideas is the way that your meaning and instinct for a piece of work will develop, however much or little you wrest conscious awareness from spontaneity.

It is a myth that having a plan always speeds writers up. Bryony Lavery is not only one of our most imaginative British playwrights – she is also one of our most prolific. She sees no point in writing if you have it all planned out in advance.

> 'Trust that you are the only story-making species in the natural world...and that your brain and heart will lead you to the next beat of your story and the one after that and the one after that...and will get very impatient with you if you don't knit and re-knit it into a good story.'

The more we trust ourselves as storytellers, the more we will entertain ourselves and others with what we discover as we write. If we cry, laugh, get angry, scared, aroused when we write, so may our audience-reader.

Philip Ridley has had award-winning careers writing children's books, plays and screenplays. He explains his process:

> 'I don't really plan anything when I'm writing. It's one of the reasons I've so rarely done a commission. I can't really tell you what a project is going to be before I've written it. A play or novel usually takes me by surprise. For me, preparation – the way something comes together – is like an explosion in reverse. You know when you see reverse film footage of something being blown up. You start with all this scattered detritus all over the place. All this shrapnel. And then this shrapnel starts to come together. That bit over there connects to this bit here. Until, eventually, you have this whole thing in front of you. Well, that's what creating something tends to be like for me. I don't know what it all means. I don't even try to think about what it all means. I just gather and ponder and start dreaming. And then…something starts to happen. A few of the collected shrapnels start to connect. That line of dialogue belongs to that character over there. That character with the dialogue belongs in that room. This is not a linear process. There's no logic to it. But once something does start to connect – and it feels right – then connections start to be made all over the place. What's more, everything I see and hear seems to fit into the thing that's forming. I can't turn on the telly without seeing a news report that has something to do with the shape that's evolving out of the shrapnel. And when all the shrapnel has joined together – you have your thing. Your project. Your new nest. A shrapnel nest. But you didn't know what type of nest you were gonna build at the beginning. Or if, indeed, it would become a nest at all. You just found yourself collecting all the shiny shrapnel that, for some reason, attracted you.'

My sense is that creative minds naturally work in this non-linear way. Phil also describes that amazing phenomenon we all experience when we're working on projects and see examples or aspects of it everywhere. When I studied neuroscience and creativity, I discovered that this isn't just zeitgeist. It's because your selection has triggered the bit of your brain called the Reticular Activating System. Not knowing the difference between fact and fiction, your RAS will draw your attention to what your mind is searching for. Test it out for yourself for a few hours – try the colour pink or signs of war or kind deeds or whatever you're already working on. Even if you only have a tiny 'what if...?' or an image or a theme or a snippet of dialogue to start with, it is as if suddenly the whole universe validates and supports your imagination. The more open and organic your process, the greater the scope. Who needs outlines, when the world is working with you?

Trusting your instincts

This whole book is about trusting your instincts as a writer. It would be lovely if everyone in a position to commission you could be persuaded to trust those instincts too. Sometimes, if you explain your needs, as Dennis and Matt describe above, commissioners will be flexible, but that takes a lot of confidence when you're starting out. Some producers simply look at risk mitigation from the wrong end. Yes, occasionally an artist won't deliver, but that's true whatever the process. Most artists create their best work when they feel trusted and safe. Writers must be free to explore and make their own rules – no one can play to order.

In my experience...

Anthony Neilson is another of the UK's finest playwrights. He is now commissioned by major companies (such as the RSC, National Theatre of Scotland, Royal Court) but there was a time, not so very long ago, when theatres wouldn't commission his work because although they loved his writing, they were too nervous of his process. Anthony would start rehearsal with a sense of his story concept – maybe only three lines. He would write during the rehearsal period. The actors effectively became his source material and dramaturgical testing ground. During this time, my company, The Red Room, commissioned and produced *The Night Before Christmas* (1995), *The Censor* (1997) and *Stitching* (2002) – all created in this way. They are regularly revived. The latter two received major awards and are modern classics.

I'm not being mystical or romantic about it, but reducing writing to a conscious craft is simply inaccurate. All writers use organic and structured processes in their work. How, when and why has to be your choice, it is unique to you. There always comes a point in the process when you find yourself examining your story but for some of you nothing beats the thrill, the rollercoaster ride, the risk of writing without a map. If the writing process is pre-determined, where's the fun in that?

RULE BREAKER 6

The journey your imagination chooses is the way

RULE 7

Write what the market wants

Any discussion of your work by prospective commissioners will be as much about potential sales as the perceived quality of your writing. The marketplace is constantly changing and it's up to commissioners to predict trends and create new ones. Unknown writers who tail trends are the least likely writers to succeed. In general, you break in as a writer because you have something new to offer the market.

Publishers and producers are forever seeking new ways to engage audiences, and digital technology has revolutionized approaches to share the powerful human experience you've created. However, because developing a market involves more creativity and capacity than tailing one, in theatre where budgets and audiences are relatively small, it can be surprisingly hard to persuade producers that a new idea is valid and calls for a fresh approach. The result is a disjuncture between the independence of much new theatre writing and the mainstream way in which it is sold. There is a strong tendency for the funded buildings to tail the market whilst writers and small companies create the conditions for new kinds of dialogue.

To some extent this is also true of film and publishing where the DIY culture is ceaselessly inventive and fleet of foot. Nonetheless, the more independent companies can be surprisingly risk averse and predictable. The interesting work is often at the edges, but because the rules of production and distribution are changing so fast those experiments could well be tomorrow's mainstream, and the independents trying to play big could find themselves out of business.

TV sees itself as market led. It can be conservative and formulaic but it is also honest about being a mass media aimed at millions. It tails other media in terms of content and whilst there are brilliant UK dramas, mainstream output is also full of quality work that takes no real risks. Were the same kind of risks permitted in drama as with children's programmes or late night comedy, TV might become a more exciting place to play.

Lucy Prebble has been hugely successful in both theatre and TV, writing hit show *Enron* (2009) and *Secret Diary of a Call Girl* (2007-11). I asked her about the differences between the two mediums and under what conditions you could break the rules in TV.

'I think my experience has been that the difference between telly and theatre is that both claim they desperately want you to challenge and break the rules associated with form and content. But that only theatre really means it. There are far more rules that are 'understood' in TV, i.e. a BBC 1 audience cannot be exposed to sex, violence or particular sorts of humour because they don't like it. As if audiences belong to a channel rather than flicking through and picking and choosing. I think the 'understood' nature of many of these TV rules does eventually beat originality out of writers (for example, you begin to understand that certain things are never financially or tonally possible so you don't write them anymore). As always, the most dangerous form of censorship in a free society is self-censorship and in this country there has never felt like a challenging, rule-breaking British drama pedigree for my generation of writers. Most references are American drama or British comedy. In *Secret Diary* I was not allowed to have the length of episode I wanted (1 hour) nor to tackle the themes or storylines I wanted to e.g. mental health issues, because they were felt to be too dark or challenging for the channel. That's why I walked off the show for the second series. Those rules weren't put there harshly or aggressively, they were always broached with an apologetic smile but a sense of "this is how it is".'

If you want to play the market

- Know your genre and/or your niche and your target audience-reader. Get to know everything that exists in the area that is your specialism and keep that audience-reader in mind as you write.
- Create your own following through a blog or social networks. Self-promote in an interesting way and people will want to read your work.
- Look outside your own specialism – find innovative ways to combine other genres/niches with your own. Keep a step ahead of your audience-reader and their circles of influence.
- Find champion directors, writers, bloggers to endorse your work.

Write for yourself

The thing is that all this stuff about writing for a market is second-guessing nonsense. You are going to write at your best when you write for yourself in the broadest sense. You might be secretly writing for an ex-lover, against an injustice or for the future. You might be writing for an imagined audience-reader with a sense of how to destabilize or delight them. But if you write to pander to existing taste or churn out stuff you don't believe in because you think it will please people, it is likely to be crap and unlikely to sell. I always feel like a piece of writing has a soul so the lack of a soul deadens my own. Of course some writers can turn their craft to something they don't feel. Some can even make us believe them. They see writing as a job where the compromises are like any other and they do it pragmatically, with detachment and professionalism.

Of course you have to eat. You can't make a living as a playwright today, unless, like Lucy Prebble, you have written a critically acclaimed West End hit and sold the film rights, or like playwright Mark Ravenhill, your work is widely and continuously produced internationally. I've seen talented playwrights sucked into TV jobs for reasons of finance or frustration and watched them jump through hoops of fire until the project they'd only half-felt in the first place became unrecognisable and they were left miserable. They were not the writers for that task. I've also seen good playwrights, who struggled in theatre, thrive in TV. Writers don't have to excel in every medium and context. The glorious thing about writing (or any art form) is that as long as you can always face yourself and your imagination, it is regenerative.

The most exciting writers don't tail the market, they create it. They break rules, no one understands them and then suddenly their way of doing things is everywhere. I think of Quentin Tarantino's *Pulp Fiction* (1994); Kathy Acker's *Blood and Guts in High School* (1984); Anthony Neilson's *Penetrator* (1993), for example, and how exhilarated I felt, the first time I encountered those works.

Timing is as important as talent, so you just have to hope that your work fits the zeitgeist and will fly. Being out of time may not mean that you're past it, it can also mean that you're ahead of your time, seeing something others aren't ready to take on board yet. Or it might be both. Ideas are recycled and time isn't linear.

Everyone wants a different experience and every piece of writing is unique. Your audience is out there somewhere whether it's just your mum or millions. Only you can know your strengths and what you enjoy writing. Hopefully other people out there will connect with that.

RULE BREAKER 7

Create the market for your work. You are the market too.

Rules 8-21

Principles or Prescriptions? Story, Character, Dialogue

Are storytelling principles immutable? Can act divisions help or hinder? How do you create shape through metaphor? Are conventions about generating character and dialogue helpful to a writer, or are they just mental clutter?

RULE 8

'Story is about principles not rules'

Robert McKee, *Story*

What makes a sequence of events a story? Are there principles to storytelling which, if they are not adhered to, destroy the notion of story altogether? If stories are universal why do we tell them and what do they mean to us?

The interest in the way stories are constructed has become a major industry. The quote above is the first line of Robert McKee's bestselling screenwriting guide *Story* (1998) which is on the reading list of journalists and business leaders as well as writers.

Screenwriter Greg Dinner voices what many writers feel about the book:

> 'I always tell my students 'McKee's very helpful. Pay close attention and then forget it.' Firstly, writing in TV and film is mostly collaborative and you don't always have much say in the process, secondly there are no hard and fast rules about structure, lastly you need to digest the rules then throw away the rule book and write who you are.'

I always liked McKee's description of story as the conflict between subjective expectation and objective reality, the gap opening between what you think will happen and what does. Although this sounds obvious, mastery of it seems to be the key to all storytelling. In the gap there is every level of conflict. Each action the character takes to close the gap creates ever greater risk. I find it hard to imagine breaking this principle and still telling a story.

Without the opening of this gap, isn't there simply boredom or overload?

I asked Greg what he thought the fundamentals of story were.

> 'There needs to be a sense of journey and that is more about a character striving towards something than any plot mechanism. This is an emotional thing too, both for the audience who is being engaged to feel something and the writer who comes to a greater knowledge of themselves through emotional involvement in their story. Character is definitely more important to story than structure. The most important structure really is the moral framework which is why I make more use of Aristotle's *Politics* than his *Poetics* when I teach screenwriting. It is the role of all writers to manipulate this structure, either upholding the status quo or challenging it.'

Greg's approach to film structure mirrors my own in theatre. We know that stories are bearers of values. When we read, we interpret the meaning of a story and when we write, we create meaning. Certain writing jobs are both interpretive and creative.

Why do we need stories?

Anthropologists think that stories first came about to serve a function of communicating the social/cultural values of a group, including geographic or food gathering knowledge. We know that the unconscious is more powerful than the conscious mind and that stories appeal to our emotions, to our deepest fears and desires. Through stories, meaning is retained at a deeper level of memory.

I think the most important aspect of stories is that they teach us how to embrace change. Stories show us that we must resist attack but that we cannot do so imperviously. We must change ourselves, adapt to new circumstances or be destroyed. This is the basis of all evolution. Stories are at the heart of how we understand ourselves in the world.

If we don't share stories (and some of us feel if we don't write down those stories), we have an uneasy sense of jeopardizing our future. So when we hear the voices we write them down just as fast as our pens or keyboards can keep up. Creativity comes from a primal place. Children beg for stories and eagerly tell them too. Every known culture has stories which shape and are shaped by its people; yet across cultures, the deepest myths repeat. Psychoanalysts such as Carl Jung have viewed this as evidence of our 'collective unconscious'.

Myths appear to come from deep in our psyche but they are also ideologically inscribed. Joseph Campbell in *The Hero with a Thousand Faces* outlines a universal story model. The main character starts in an 'ordinary world', as Christopher Vogler calls it. At first the hero refuses the call to adventure but eventually takes the decision to cross the threshold into the 'special world' on a quest. Here he must actively invest in the outcome of the story because the stakes are high, often life or death. When he has risen to the challenge and succeeded, he claims his reward and (usually) takes it home.

This mythic journey is reminiscent of the Aboriginal separation-initiation-return ritual. The young boy goes on walkabout in the wild to find another tribe, to be given its story as reward and then return home a man. Jung might say that the Great Snake hungrily awaiting the boy who is about to be circumcised is an image that is part of our collective unconscious. Some radical anthropologists argue that this very initiation right was a political freeing from the mother-bond, a repeated overthrowing of women's once central role.[5] In this paradigm, there was originally a version of these stories with a female-centred mythology that was stolen and reworked by the men. We know that Aboriginal women could be gang raped to death if they tried to discover the men's stories. Stories make and remake us. To own the story is to have power.

As Richard Dawkins explained to us, we are the only species that can overturn the rule of our 'selfish' genes.[6] We can act collaboratively, consciously and for the good of a future we may never see. Storytelling seems a vital link between our ability to talk and our ability to work together. When we stop competing, we exchange and share and therein lies the possibility of progressive change. Withholding the narrative then setting it free has helped us survive as human beings and given us the ability to turn what exists and what doesn't into a whole collective alternative to what is. Like other aspects of our survival – eating, drinking and sexual reproduction – stories also give us pleasure.

The meaning of stories can emerge from compassion or cruelty, but if compassion is not apparent from the storyteller towards the story, generally the story will not be believed. What evokes compassion, like what evokes fear, depends on the context.

In 2010, on the day of the general election, I saw a matinee performance of Laura Wade's superb attack on the violence and immunity of privilege in *Posh* at the Royal Court Theatre. The play follows an evening with the barbaric 'Riot Club' (based on the student Bullingdon Club of which David Cameron, now Prime Minister and Boris Johnson, Mayor of London were both members). The Royal Court sits in Sloane Square, one of the poshest areas of London. I was fascinated and a little frightened at the gulf between my laughter points and the laughter of the majority of the audience who appeared to identify with the murderous upper-class characters.

I felt a different kind of cultural divide watching Olivier runner-up and Alfred Fagon Award-winner *Iya Ile* (2009) by Oladipo Agboluaje, which we co-produced with Tiata Fahodzi at Soho Theatre. It attracted an audience that included many middle-class Nigerians. Laughter and horror revealed itself differently in this audience too, depending on many cultural/political references, among other things, whether or not you had grown up in a household where having/beating servants was viewed as normal.

When a work is freed from mainstream thought, there tends to be a greater breadth of opinion around it. This might include making explicit the ideological premise of the work, as in the two plays above, rather than hiding that premise or pretending that it doesn't exist.

Getting lost on your writer's journey

One of the biggest paradoxes about writing stories, is that we can never get as close to ourselves in reality as we can through illusion, through the voices of 'the others'. Through fiction you are permitted to speak the unspeakable through the mouths of your characters, to explore the edge of behaviour, a heightened, more adventurous version of reality, where each moment sings with meaning. It's thrilling to invent new worlds and to experience them. It's hugely pleasurable to explore the wildest world of your imagination whilst remaining physically safe. Like being in a dream that you know is a dream, however lost in the dream world you are, ultimately you can make the return to reality.

Sometimes you forget that this is true, your special world completely takes over. The world that you are lost in bleeds through into the objective world, RAS kicks in (**Rule 6**) and you see references to your imaginary world everywhere. This validates the primacy of your fiction, keeps you feeling more authentic there than in a less intense reality. On the other hand, you might have reached for fiction to escape the intensity of your life, to lighten the load. You too may have a feeling of being outside of the real world when you return.

At Soho Theatre I had the pleasure of programming Spill Festival, which brought us a delicious Forced Entertainment show called *Void Story* (2009) by Tim Etchells. Unlike most of Forced Ents' work it is not fragmented from many points of view, but instead is one hurtling, high-speed, apocalyptic narrative lurching from disaster to disaster, like a cartoon nightmare testing hopefulness in the face of being kidnapped, bombed, stabbed, run over, poisoned, murdered and brutalized in all manner of ways. It is a farcical rather than believable story but the tragedy seeps through and it becomes emotionally cathartic – or at least that was my experience. We find ourselves identifying with two flat characters in an unbelievable world. I think this is because though the lurches of narrative feel untrue, the horrors of their world are our own, and we identify with the passive characters who, in the face of disaster, refuse to die or submit, but just keep going, taking on the horrors faced by millions in reality every day. For more on passive characters see **Rule 15**.

Screenwriter Terry Hodgkinson trained as a painter and was first encouraged to write by director Fred Zinnemann when he was working for him as an assistant director. He never looked back.

> 'I went to one of Robert McKee's expensive seminars in London, years ago, but he just confirmed what I already knew, it's all just logic and common sense. If the story entertains, you've got it. If it's boring, start again.'

RULE BREAKER 8

You create principles through story

RULE 9

If you would have your play deserve success, Give it five acts complete; nor more, nor less;

Horace, *Ars Poetica* (c.18 BCE)[7]

Horace took credit for inventing the five-act play so he would say that. The turning points became the breaks when the amphitheatre audiences stretched their legs, had a drink and a chat. Nowadays, there may be commercial breaks on TV, but in a five act film, for example, the act breaks are not marked but played straight through. So what purpose do they serve?

Well, for most writers, breaking down the natural movement of a story into sequences makes it easier to write those transitions which define the end of one section of the story and launch you into the next. You may also want to group certain series of events together into their own story arc and mood. This can help link the subplot to the main plot, for example, or allow the progression of one character's journey in a multiplot. It's rarer to find acts in modern plays, though sometimes there are grouped scenes. Three acts are more common in film these days and four or five acts to TV. In the novel, a chapter sometimes contains a sequence of many scenes, more akin to an act. However, these are all loose trends – as we know there are no rules.

The five-act structure has had a renaissance in BBC soaps. Shakespeare is generally evoked to prove its universality, though whether or not the Bard wrote in five acts is a moot point. We do know that he wrote quickly and for continuous action and if he literally wrote in five acts, which many doubt, he did so inconsistently. The fact that many of his plays yield well to a five act structure is probably because he was familiar with it and wrote with an innate sense of storytelling.[†] If beginning, middle and end leaves you with just too much middle to manipulate, then you may prefer to break a three-act structure into five. I'm making delineations sound random, which they aren't, but they can only be defined by the needs of your material and process.

Just so we're clear on what we're talking about, I have outlined a story structure on the following pages. It is broken down into a skeletal five-act structure, with a three-act structure in brackets and an eight-sequence structure also indicated. To add in Truby's twenty-two steps would be too much for the scope of this little section[8] but I hope it's clear that a classic story arc may be broken down in different ways and will rhythmically change as a result of the way it is segmented.

Keeping it organic

All of these story designs emphasize an inverse symmetry, as if the *midpoint* were a mirror. Of course many stories will not follow this structure, but it is a common basis for a lot of films, TV dramas and plays. Novels, being bigger, may have many more twists and turns to the story.

You will see that being favoured by Hollywood does not make the three act structure any more universal than the five act.

[†]   Shakespeare would have learnt the five-act structure at school from Terence and we know that he later read, ripped off and improved upon Seneca. There is no evidence that he literally used five acts – in the way that Ben Jonson did for example. There is evidence of act breaks with musical interludes being introduced for the first time when his company moved to Blackfriars Theatre in 1609. It's likely that act breaks were imposed on Shakespeare's plays in the Folio edition, published in 1623, seven years after his death, though not with complete consistency here either. Folio publication was rare for plays and perhaps acts elevated the work to classical status. Ben Jonson had a hand in the Folio too.

FIVE-ACT, THREE-ACT AND EIGHT-SEQUENCE STRUCTURE

BEGINNING

Problem	World changes	Awareness

Act 1 (Act 1)

1. Her world – her status quo. Possible sense of her denial/ fear of something.

2. Change happens to rock her world *(Inciting Incident)* and forces her to (re)act. She now has a goal and she knows what's in her way. What could be simpler?

MIDDLE

Seeking solution	She changes	Complication

Act 2 (Act 2)

3. She tries to achieve her goal, but she underestimates her antagonists and makes the situation worse. She makes new friends and enemies.

Act 3 (Act 2)

4. She devises a new strategy. However, her previous actions have complicated things. She faces her shadow self, her unconscious need and realizes she will have to fundamentally change to sort things out. *(Midpoint – point of no return)*

5. She starts to change to deal with the complication and is partly successful as a result. She faces a test that confirms what she's up against. She may falter and doubt her new changed self and start to return to her old patterns. Can she sustain this change and will it work?

Act 4 (Act 2)

6. The harder she tries, the more obstacles emerge, testing her commitment to the full. She considers abandoning her goal. Then she is confronted by a seemingly insurmountable obstacle. Reunion with self or revelation about why she is striving for this. She now faces her greatest danger/ opportunity; low/high point; wound/human potential *(Crisis)*. She chooses what action to take. Can she succeed in defeating antagonists, internal and external?

END

| Solution | She changes world | Resolution |

Act 5 (Act 3)

7. She triumphs/fails – takes/loses prize *(Climax)*

8. She has changed. The world has changed. Maybe she has even changed the world. *(Resolution)*

Many different act designs can be grafted onto a classic story and used to mark out its dramatic arc in a particular way. One writer said that when he was in Hollywood he was given an acetate sheet with plot points corresponding to page numbers and told to follow it. What could be more deadening to creativity than that?

Another screenwriter, Chris Lunt says:

> 'It wasn't until I was halfway through a re-draft of my most recent script bar one that I heard the term 'inciting incident' or the idea of a 'five-act format'. The truth is, if you study film you'll naturally fall into these patterns without overly planning to do so. That's not a bad thing, it's a bad thing when you put the format cart before the creative horse. More importantly, I'd work on developing a 'voice' regardless of the genre you're writing.'

We are all familiar with certain story forms and naturally repeat them. If it helps you to think about your story arc in terms of specific acts or sequences or steps, then go for it. However, we shouldn't mistake conventions for deep meaning or think that it is the acts themselves that generate organic structure. The biggest problem with thinking in acts is that it can lock you into something less original than you would otherwise write. We have an intrinsic sense of how story works and we need to free ourselves to invent the shape that emerges from the material we're developing. It's all up for grabs (see **Rule 10**).

Formal experimentation is common amongst new writers, partly from an ignorance of the rules and also from a genuine excitement about the potential of their medium (**Rule 22**). Screenwriter Stephen Brady explained how one of his first screenplays broke the classic structural rules.

> 'I wrote it deliberately without inciting incident. It was about an alcoholic and I wanted it to have a structure which reflected his life, freewheeling and shapeless. I have often wondered whether it would have actually been

produced if I had written a more conventional structure and I often think of going back to it. The problem is, I think that producers size up a project against the rule book in their head rather than ask the more important question 'What am I getting instead?'

The 'rule book in the head' describes well the unimaginative gatekeeper, but there is also a rule book in every writer's head. We need bravery and self-awareness to break with that.

Thinking in sequences of change

All stories are made up of sequences of change. In prose fiction, scenes are generally freer because of interior monologue and narrative. A scene is usually unified by time and place. The defining aspect of any scene or sequence is that something changes from beginning to end and the story of that change mainly happens in the middle – a kind of structural microcosm of the whole. At the climactic turning point in a scene you may pull away to create more tension rather than resolve it, launching us into the next section of the work.

Dynamising your scenes

Scenes can literally fall flat. A lack of dynamic, engaging movement is usually down to one or more of the following:

- The scene hasn't turned. What that means is that there has been no reversal or major advance from the beginning of the scene to the end. Nothing has changed in story terms. For example, if your main character has entered the scene wanting to make things up with his lover, for the scene to turn we must feel that the odds of him succeeding have changed by the end, or that some greater priority has taken over. In other words, in pursuing his goal for the scene, he succeeds, fails or changes his mind.
- Check that the moment of change has been allowed to land. Your audience-reader needs to feel it. Often you can

identify one line or action as the turning point. Usually in screenwriting and prose fiction you need to write the reaction to this turn. In theatre it tends to be implicit because we can see all the players in a scene.

- You may have achieved a turning point in your scene but it still falls flat because it's of the wrong scale or intensity or is repetitious. It doesn't progress the conflict and/or it doesn't seem plausible. Remember that your scene is a story with stakes rising towards a turning point. A turn also happens more subtly within every beat of the scene (see page 113), in the same way that all the scenes progress to the turning point of the whole story.

- Check that everything is changing with cause, that it's earning its place. Try playing out the scene to find where the glitch is. Solutions may include opening/closing a story gap; totally rewriting it from another perspective or changing the situation or setting.

- Scenes aren't always a win-lose scenario. As in life, you can have win-win or lose-lose, but it rarely advances main character conflict. Usually it's reserved for generating fresh complication through minor or comedy characters or for resolving a sequence of events. Exceptions to this include when both sides set aside their conflict to unite against a third party or when it is revealed to them (by one another perhaps) that the situation is different to what they thought.

- Predictability is a major cause of flatness. Things need to get better or worse or even better or even worse but good or bad news thrice in a row in serious drama will feel like a cliché and can only serve a comic purpose. The ups and downs of life need to be true from beat to beat as well as through the progression of scenes. So check that from the point of view of your main character things shift unpredictably. For example, he loses one beat and wins the next two, even if one of those wins is a false positive. If that makes it sound like a game, that's not a bad way to think about it. Sometimes you can cut out of a scene early to enable a reversal of fortunes. It's the peaks and troughs that compel us to keep engaging. Negative reversals can be subtle of course. For example, an overconfident character may climb progressively higher, excitedly over-riding negative signals, but those reversals must still be there for us to believe his journey.

- Check that the main character has a clear goal and an unconscious need and that the obstacles are not too weak or overwhelming and are creating conflict on multiple levels.
- Too many competing conflicts and the story becomes confused. Be clear about your conflict priorities, and whose story and/or point of view we're looking from. Streamline a little. It's a story, not real life.

In film, a scene may be only one beat long. In theatre there may be no separate scenes at all if you have unity of time and place, but you will still find yourself creating the equivalent of scenes by building the action towards turning points which you might classically punctuate by entrances and exits (French scenes) or by stage action. A novel may be without chapters but it will still have its rhythm and dynamic. However formal the divisions to any text, they mark out a world of change. It's up to you how you design the audience-reader's experience.

RULE BREAKER 9

Use the sequences of change that best express your story

RULE 10

Structure is what holds it all together

A whole is what has a beginning and middle and end...

Aristotle

...a beginning, a middle and an end but not necessarily in that order

Jean Luc Godard

Let's say that the story structure described in **Rule 9**, the traditional hero's journey, doesn't best express your feelings for the material. How do you go about exploring other options and feeling confident to follow your own instincts?

What is structure?

Many screenwriting gurus talk about structure as if it were a kind of container holding all elements of the work together or like a house inside which the characters live. These kind of metaphors feel alien to me. Yes, I can look at structure in that way and some writers find that useful. But I don't *experience* structure that way. It's not how I feel the inner heartbeat or meaning of a piece of work. Emotional shape is the key and that comes from within the life of the story.

Structure is not something separate from a piece of work. It is intrinsic to it. In fact shape might be a better word than structure, or maybe movement, not forward momentum necessarily, more in the sense of resonance. Of course, I'm the first to point out to a writer that a scene doesn't turn or there's a missing beat or let's not introduce that subplot so late or what happens if we change the chronology of those events. This is my job, to achieve a desired *emotional* impact, a movement which you can only understand by working feelingly from inside a piece of writing.

Our inadequate shorthand language for structure describes the primal movement at work in a story. The internal dynamic of a piece of writing is below the surface and it seems to me to derive initially from the way that you as a writer hold and nurture the work in yourself, from those beginnings of feelings, images, snatches of voice, to the sense of story building in life and momentum. In my experience it is this *holding* of the story as a kind of living creature that best describes my sense of what structure is. This may be partly due to my background in theatre, where collaboration with actors and the audience plays such a public role in shaping the work. Notwithstanding fixed cues, choreography, or the precision of emotional beats – if the piece is alive and the audience awake, the structure will be different every night.

When I read a new play, I read in one sitting as if I were its audience. I read as if the play were onstage. I also read from inside the perspectives of the characters and their world. I read the way I dream. A sense of place and time is crucial to this. I mustn't separate the work from the writer yet, there is a bonding still occurring and the work is still growing. The performed shape grows out of this approach to the work as something living, feeling, a world in the process of transformation. I may work through any number of drafts with a writer, usually no more than ten, before it becomes a collaboration with other artists and audiences.

In a novel, the structure is freer to roam in a different way – inside the minds of the characters for example, inside the mind of the reader who can choose to reread a paragraph three times before moving on. Language is fundamental to this. You write in pictures, we read those pictures in words and see our own pictures as we do. In film, the story is led by pictures not words and on cinema release at least, the structure is locked down and intended to be seen in one sitting.

Metaphor as structure

Amanda Holiday, screenwriter and artist, suggests using pictograms to represent the structure of a work – simple diagrams or images that express the theme and metaphor.

> 'Scriptwriting is often piecemeal, bitty – and, caught up in the writing, it's easy to lose sight of the whole – particularly if it hasn't been resolved from the outset. Sometimes the difficult part is actually 'writing out' the way the story fits together – even after it has been 'resolved' in the mind. Maybe the film's central metaphor is there and for the writer, that's enough to be going on with. As Paul Schrader said 'metaphor is the structure.'

Metaphor is a high impact, economical approach to structure. For example, Philip Ridley's *Leaves of Glass*, also works structurally through a series of metaphors – in this case of capitalism, denier of history, rushing headlong into crisis. We experience disordered fragmentary family encounters full of lies, the erasure of a child's key horrific memory of being prostituted by his older brother. Phil explains his approach to metaphoric structure.

> 'I sometimes see writing a play as the hunt for the correct architecture of images. Images and colours and objects. Each character has their own 'imagist' way of speaking. Through the journey of the play these images are riffed on, they become distorted, they metamorphose into something else. The images of one character are picked up by another character, and a third set of images are formed. This 'image architecture' is the emotional dreamtime of the play. An audience is, hopefully, picking up on them, but not with the front part of their brain. It's something going on in their subconscious. This is nothing new, of

course. All plays do this to a greater or lesser extent. I only mention it because a lot of people have picked up on this and have said, 'Oh, it must be because he trained as a painter. That's why he likes these images so much.' But that is not the case. The images in my plays do not feel like painterly images to me. They feel like...well, they feel like theatrical images. If you asked me to explain the difference I don't think I could. But there is a difference. I think it's something to do with the use of metaphor. In theatre, the metaphor of an image works in a more accumulative way. An image in a painting is about that image. But an image in a stage play is about who is saying it and how it relates to all the other images in the play. In many ways, theatrical images are more like images in cinema. They are about keeping the emotional journey thrusting forward. What's this image about? It's about the next image.'

Iraqi film-maker Maysoon Pachachi told me about her latest project, a screenplay called *Nothing doing in Baghdad*. Though Maysoon lives in the UK, she has spent much time in Baghdad since the war began, setting up a film school to enable the training of film-makers to continue there and also to support the documentation of life for ordinary Iraqis. She felt it would be false and wrong in her own screenplay to use the hero model of structure to reflect lives that were so fragmented now and 'impossible'. She didn't want her film to be 'turned into a product that could be put on a shelf and forgotten.'

Roy Williams also feels that political urgency can impact on structure, that the context and material must determine the approach. This happened with his own play about the Iraq war.

'Too much structuring can hold a playwright back. When I was writing *Days Of Significance*, I felt speed was of the essence. The pace of the play seemed to demand that. Structuring the play went right out of the window. I just wrote, scenes and more scenes, trusting that the characters as well as the piece would take me where I needed to go. Structure can find itself without me interfering with it.'

In Roy's case this new freedom came from a mastery of storytelling and led to one of his finest plays.

Time/Chronology

Stories are either linear, where the story moves forward in its own real time following one or more characters from beginning to end, or non-linear, where the story deviates from the straightforward path and our sense of time is less about where we're going than what connects us – across, with or against time. Often writers use elements of linear and non-linear in the same work.

For you as an active audience-reader, chronology is linear even when the work isn't. So there is always a relationship between your real time and the work. At one extreme they are the same. In Philip Ridley's *Piranha Heights* (2008), for example, the intensity for the audience watching states of psychotic shock was heightened by the play's unity of time, place and action, fairly unusual in contemporary theatre. Our traverse production increased the traumatic sensation of entrapment.

You lose your awareness of time when absorbed in a piece. Your relationship with a work may also be temporally disrupted, as for example when you fall asleep and wake up again during a film or have to get off the tube in the middle of a chapter. When we feel there is a missing beat to the story or a piece too many, it can also impact on how we experience time. We'll search in vain and then feel loss or frustration or a sense of time dragging. Time stops being in the moment and we stop believing.

It's always worth giving your work's relationship to time deep consideration and specifically how temporal life and chronology express the needs of your material. I remember in the very first draft of Kay Adshead's *The Bogus Woman* (2000), the Young Woman's memory of persecution back home moved forward with the same chronology as her journey in the UK to Campsfield Detention Centre. This meant that the first action of the play was the most brutal and unspeakable, the massacre of her family and newborn baby. The problem was that everything after this became anti-climactic and the ill-treatment of the Young Woman at the hands of the British authorities seemed like nothing to what she had suffered 'back home.'

In reality, victims of torture experience post-traumatic stress, they fear being sent back and have a host of psychological symptoms that experts in the field can explain. In story terms, however, if we see horror inflicted on a character, we feel more compassion if we know them first. On the level of story meaning, the Young Woman's memories of horrific events back home worked better in reverse, peeling back towards the unspeakable massacre. This is the final 'flashback'. The protest at Campsfield Detention Centre then dramatically becomes a release of anger and trauma. In changing this one aspect of chronology, Kay linked British asylum policy to the trauma suffered before arrival and emotionally persuaded the audience that the UK system was unjust and inhumane.

Some common shapes in relation to time

As I have tried to indicate, any kind of structure or process is up for grabs to achieve your desired impact. Below, I attempt to describe the relationship of certain shapes to time. The terminology is my own or it is generic. You may have your own words for something similar. It doesn't really matter how you name or categorise these common shapes/approaches, nor would an exhaustive list be possible. They might be used in combination or contribute to another kind of shape. They are in no way prescriptive, just listed to express that there are endless possibilities and ways to describe what we call 'structure'.

Dialectic return. The story moves dialectically, returning to the same point at a higher or deeper level. Often the point is a contested memory or ideology, e.g. *Memento, We Need to Talk About Kevin, Leaves of Glass, The Measures Taken.*

Associative. Time is more surreal, works through a new dream time logic that we learn as we go. More like a 'join the dots' pattern than directional. For example, *Alice's Adventures in Wonderland* or *Un Chien Andalou*, the final image of which Beckett used to start his play *Happy Days* with Winnie, just like the couple at the end of Buñuel's film, up to her waist in sand.

Parallel worlds/Multi-plot. May use different places or time frames to show any number of different stories. Stories may connect directly or not, e.g. *The Hours, Far Away, The Slap, Hoxton Story.* A multi-plot generally has juxtaposed stories feeding into a bigger story and the main character in one story may be an antagonist or supporter in another. With parallel worlds, the link may be thematic rather than through character journeys. Another version is the **Branching story** – everything branches out from the spine of the story, adding more 'twigs' or details to each branch as it is explored. Often used with multi-plot stories such as *Pulp Fiction* (uses frames, three-act structure and an appearance of simultaneity too). The internet is a kind of open-ended branching narrative (see **Hypertext** below). Parallel worlds and, below, Dual/Duel, are not the same as subplot by definition, though of course it might be argued that all stories with one subplot contain at least three stories.

Dual/Duel. A version of the above with two stories which may or may not compete for meaning. When they do, the result can be disturbing and psychotic, as used to great effect in the film *A Beautiful Mind*, in which we do not realise for some time that we are watching hallucinations. The stories may be in the present or mix time frames or do both. I commissioned Anthony Neilson's play *Stitching* because of the emotional impact of its extraordinary structural twist whereby the audience is led to believe they are watching flashback scenes from the past that will lead us to a better understanding of the present. In fact we are watching scenes from the future (i.e. the present) when the child from the pregnancy the couple might terminate has already lived and died. So much of Anthony's work is about subverting expectation and in this play he makes use of the audience's assumption that the first scene it sees will be in the present. In crime stories we don't have this expectation. All crime stories might be said to employ a dual structure in the sense that the first story, that of the crime, has already taken place and is uncovered through the story of the investigation.

Frames, Russian dolls, Plays within plays. One world contained inside another that frames it, as in *Caucasian Chalk Circle*, or a memory story such as *Never Let Me Go* or one story containing many stories (via flashbacks, dreams, surreal or real-time elements) such as *Baghdad Wedding*.

Simultaneous. This is possible in theatre, where you can watch or walk through simultaneous narratives. In film, split screen or cross-cutting can give a sense of this. In novels the layout of the text or invisibility of shifts can also move you through different points of view in suspended time.

Hypertext. Where a non-linear, interactive narrative is achieved through internal textual references, e.g. *Hopscotch* by Cortázar or through the potential of the internet where the reader selects what path to take through the work and even edits it e.g. *The Unknown*. In theatre a similar idea can be seen in interactive work where an audience makes a choice of which route to follow or decision to make, e.g. *Internal, Masque of the Red Death* or *A Small Town Anywhere*, all of which also use simultaneity.

The shape of things to come

Even in the last decade we can see how structural norms are changing in response to wider changes in the culture, reflected in who the audience is and what they are responding to. The internet and gaming may literally have forced the pace – readers and audiences expect speed and seem less prepared to spend time getting to know a character. The dominant culture takes more narrative swerves than it did ten years back and uses suspense or interaction more frequently as mechanisms of engagement. Of course this trend will also produce its opposite. The compression of the independent film sector in the UK and the conservatism of TV leads me to hope that a youth-led cultural revolution is around the corner. Books are swiftly disappearing, though the stories in them are not. It feels as if an entirely new form/process must soon emerge, not just a recycling or repackaging.

RULE BREAKER 10

Shape is alive and ever-changing

RULE 11

Hit the Ground Running

CLOV: Finished, it's finished, nearly finished, it must be nearly finished.

Samuel Beckett, first lines of Endgame

Everyone's time is precious in the creation of a new work, but investment is unequal. Let's imagine that you have sweated blood over your speculative script. A reader who wades through hundreds of submissions is unlikely to approach yours with the same patience and commitment you have bestowed upon it. They will read it hoping to discover an amazing new voice and setting aside questions of taste for those of time, if they are not immediately intrigued, they're likely to move on to the next prospect on the pile. The busy reader scenario simply anticipates what may happen when your writing is finally produced/published. The bored switch channels, chuck down the book or walk out of the theatre.

We know from neuroscience that our brains work best when they are forced to work more quickly. Our minds crave stimulus and challenge. So what better way to serve this than by starting your story as late as possible? It's exciting to enter mid-action, get your reader asking 'what?' and 'why?', 'who?' or 'how?' **Hit the ground running** instructs you to grab 'em in the first three pages, three beats or even three lines.

Hiding and cutting exposition

Hit the ground running is good advice for the writer who doesn't trust their reader-audience to work the story out. The set-up is important but new writers often need to be reassured that characters can reveal themselves quite satisfyingly through present action with little need for exposition. In case it's worth saying, exposition generally refers to information that isn't part of the forward momentum of the story but helps in some way to explain the story/character motivation. Backstory usually refers to a character's history before the story begins and as we saw in **Rule 9**, the most important aspect of this is usually their fear or denial – their wound (**Rules 14** and **15**).

So what do you do with necessary exposition? Well, the most sophisticated approach is to embed it within the overall story design and use it as revelation to propel new action (**Rule 26**). However, at the beginning of the story that's not always possible. You can pragmatically disguise it in realism, through a mixture of extreme economy and through scattering the information where it will not interrupt narrative flow or visibly slow the pace. So if you need a character to recall an incident with her mother, let it emerge through the action of the scene and also take the action forward. As a director of new plays, I am well used to hiding a writer's explanations and actors are skilled in this too. In rehearsal unearned exposition can become the most troublesome aspect of a new play. Lines scream at you to cut or conceal them. If you're in a non-realistic mode, you may not need to hide exposition. Instead, you decide when and how to reveal it.

In my experience...

I've heard seasoned writers advise new writers to always cut the beginning. This may often be helpful advice, but it isn't a rule – each case must be looked at concretely. It's true that the best writers will face the challenge of too much backstory from time to time simply because the work has organically evolved along a new path. I remember sitting at a script meeting with visionary Philip Ridley watching him coolly cut thirty pages from the top of *Piranha Heights*. That's artistic confidence. It was a brave decision which transformed the balance of the whole play and allowed Phil to deliver the state of shock at its most dramatic.

Conversely, before we toured *Made in England* (1998), which I commissioned and directed for the Red Room, Parv Bancil *added* a whole first act that hadn't existed when we first performed it. Being shown the backstory as present action added new meaning to the rest of the play, and through viewing the wider context of cross-generational conflict, the audience was able to empathise with all the characters.

Arousing compassion and curiosity

Though *Made in England* worked in both versions – just differently – you can see the potential drawback of starting a story mid-action. If an audience doesn't care, its curiosity is unlikely to be aroused about what happens next. In a novel, backstory may sometimes be used in the early chapters to create a deep connection with your main character. This is less likely to be the case with dramatic writing, because actors naturally create intriguing subtext, but you still need to build our empathy through action (**Rule 13**). In film, the potential of flashback or voice-over is sometimes exploited, though unless it's driving forward the action, it can feel like a cheat.

In theatre, audiences will accept a slower burn. This may be because we still watch more old plays than new and because of TV the pace of realism has quickened. On the other hand, Shakespeare and his contemporaries packed in more action than any new play. Perhaps we're also more acclimatized to what's erroneously called 'post-dramatic' theatre, which, relying less on story, can be reflective, static or subtle. More significantly, the rule of grabbing the audience by the throat feels different when you have a captive audience. As a theatre director, I can be playful with the way I begin a show; for example, expand the first ten minutes because the audience are still adjusting to immersion in a new world and looking intently for clues. They won't remember or realise the expansion of time, the 'trick', but they will gain a heightened awareness that will serve the intensity of the rest of the play. When we're slowed down, we're emotionally more vulnerable and connected. Of course such a choice will be informed by the writing.

In a novel, cheating time is intrinsic to the whole process of drawing the reader into your world. It's about keeping the story alive, in flow. Some of the most beautiful beginnings are quietly done. They draw you in to the atmosphere and emotion of a world through specific details of character(s), setting and conflict or the uniqueness of a character's point of view. The first few chapters of *This is How* (2009) by novelist M.J. Hyland exemplify this approach. She raises story questions softly, creating unease, rather than providing proofs; it is the intensity of focus, the raw intimacy and emotional detail that is so important in building the world of her hostile, fragile narrator. Check the establishment of your own fictional world for abstract or generic aspects, any 'unlived' moments. Bring to them greater concreteness, presence and individuality.

We've established that the beginning of a work can be the bit that's most rewritten or cut once the story is finished. On the other hand, I've known first scenes that never change though everything else does. Somehow it all just came together in that moment of writing, the keynote for the whole composition. Because of this, it may also be the scene that the writer is incapable of touching, in an almost superstitious sense.

Prologues

Let's imagine that you've achieved everything a beginning can. You've created care and concern for at least one significant character and their conflict; you've set the time and a strong sense of place; provoked questions and emotional connection to the world; cut or hidden exposition; created action, tension, pace. Still, it all feels a bit crammed in – too much unspoken before this point. Or perhaps there is a huge time or place difference, change of point of view or lurch in style between the first scene and the next.

Many skillful writers have used prologues to powerful effect but they are a bit of a fashion rule breaker these days, except in certain genres such as TV crime, thrillers and sci-fi, where you may want to show the murder or introduce the rules of a strange world. **Hit the ground running** can feel like more of a challenge when you're presenting us with an alternative world or an unfamiliar setting or style. How many new impressions can we absorb at once? It's worth remembering, of course, that all fictions are new worlds with their own rules.

A prologue might be used to set up the questions of the whole story and the epilogue, as in *Pulp Fiction* (1994). This is slightly different to its more common use as a framing device that justifies the storytelling, as in *The Caucasian Chalk Circle* (1948) or *The Name of the Rose* (1980). The advantage of turning your first scene into a prologue is that the reader-audience will expect a big shift rather than be put off by it. A disadvantage is that now you have to create two great beginnings instead of just one. Two chances for our hurried professional reader to sigh and move on. Just as with the opening of your main story, the prologue needs to hook us in rather than bombard us with stuff we don't care about yet. Be clear about what your unique prologue is doing there and why it can't simply be part of the whole.

The end in the beginning

Another well-used convention of beginnings is to foreshadow the end, often through a metaphor, phrase or symbolic gesture. It can be very satisfying in the final moments of the story to refer back to the start, particularly in shorter form work. It may be a symbolism that you work in later, after you've written the end, or it may be a repeated image or line of dialogue that expands outwards during the work. There are many ways to use this idea.

Hitting the ground running can offer a tough mental challenge that gets our brains whirring and our compassion can be aroused by slowing the action down. Provoke curiosity and stir empathy and you connect us with our survival instincts, including our deepest emotional states of desire and fear.

RULE BREAKER 11

Arouse compassion with a slow build

RULE 12

Know as much detail as possible about your characters

Before I write down one word, I have to have the character in my mind through and through. I must penetrate into the last wrinkle of his soul.

Henrik Ibsen[9]

This rule is intriguing and I have pondered it often over the years, in my work with actors and writers as well as in my own writing. Does inventing more details for your character than you could ever possibly use, inspire you to create more original moments when you do write? Though as audience-reader we only get to see the tip of the iceberg, do we unconsciously sense the solid mass below? Or can the groundwork get in your way as a writer, cluttering your mind with pointless details that you will never use? Does a dynamic and changeable character become, through this detailing process, too much of a fixed essence?

Though some of the questions in the exercises below relate to deep character, many of the character question lists doled out at writers' workshops are about inventing characteristics, banal preferences of the favourite colour/music/alcohol variety. Of course you want to create specific detail, but isn't necessity the mother of invention? You could fill twenty notebooks and still not know in the moment you need it whether your character flips their fried egg or whether that matters to your story.

Playwright and screenwriter Dennis Kelly creates unpredictable, memorable characters.

He offers his take on this rule:

> 'I remember talking to a young writer who was having
> a terrible problem with a character and she couldn't
> understand why as she'd done all the things she was
> supposed to, one of which was ask the character forty
> questions. It struck me that I'd never known forty things
> about any of my characters. I probably would struggle
> to tell you forty definite and true things about my best
> friends or even myself, so why should I apply something
> so pointless and peculiar to a character? To saddle this
> poor emerging writer with this arbitrary and potentially
> destructive rule seemed very confusing. I'm sure the
> person who suggested such a thing meant it in good faith,
> it might even have been something that helped them
> enormously, but the idea that it's a rule or law is wrong
> and was proving debilitating. Characters aren't constructs,
> they're people. That actually isn't true, of course they are
> constructs, of course they are not real people, but if you
> as the author can't believe in their living, breathing reality
> who else is going to?'

The first part of Dennis's quote reminds me of what Somerset
Maugham said about knowing less about people the more you get
to know them. Of course, in a certain sense, you do know your
characters better than you would a real person but they need to
be just as contradictory to be of interest. In realistic storytelling,
character contradiction has to be tempered with a sense of
consequence – too many contradictions can overcomplicate the
focus or diminish the believability of your story. If causal story
is not your concern then revel in exploring multiple identities or
decentred characters. Of course it is also possible to create realistic
characters who switch identities or perspectives in a moment –
Liam in Dennis Kelly's *Orphans* does this and has a psychopath's
ability to appear to give the other characters what they want.

Some writers create characters to serve their story. Others live
with their characters for a while, get under their skin by spending
time with them. Often the process mixes these approaches but

only when the characters feel alive can you start to write. To read or watch Ronan Bennett's work is to appreciate this – his characters are always drawn with delicacy, depth and truth.

> 'Before I can write the first scene – I mean this literally –
> I have to feel my characters are as real to me as my own
> family. I need an emotional connection to them and to
> their world before I can enter fictionally into it.'

Mike Leigh famously creates characters by working through a list of questions about their life history, their preferences, their needs, but he writes in collaboration with actors, developing the story through bringing the characters to life alone then physically putting them together. It was doing a workshop with Mike Leigh in the late 1980s that gave me the confidence to work with actors to create characters from scratch.

As writers, you can adapt this approach and explore or develop character in the same spirit of free improvisation. For those whose characters walk into their lives and create the story, this process of discovery happens naturally and it seems counter-intuitive to ask conscious questions. However, those of you who know your story and think 'what kind of character do I need for that' may find it very helpful as a process. In an open exploration you could start with 'facts' such as full name, age, birthplace, physical features and move onto more subjective questions, such as those below, but importantly all of it is provisional. At the core of Mike Leigh's approach was the vital coaching 'if you don't know the answer, make it up.' This is the key to its empowerment. I'd add, 'if you don't care about the question, move on.' For even less conscious responses, work against the clock or accept what comes first as you would with automatic writing. Questions for your character can be focused or random, broad or detailed. This exercise can be done as a writing or mulling exercise, just sitting with your character and observing their responses.

The following questions are just a tiny example of stimuli to blank canvas character creation. Obviously the possibilities are endless.

- What was her favourite subject at school and why?
- What is he most proud of having achieved and why?
- What did her father/sister/gran always say to her?
- What's the worst sex she ever had?
- What's his idea of a perfect day?
- How did he feel when he was last hugged?
- What does she feel would be the worst thing someone could say about her?
- What does he think stopped him being the person he wanted to be?

Or you might let your character complete sentences such as

- I used to believe that…
- I hated it when…
- I had to laugh when…
- If money was no object I would…

Or let your character riff in response to a word from a random or designed list just to spark a fresh detail or idea.

Whisky	Friendship	Blanket
Eco-warrior	Jaguar	Poland

My only indispensable character list comprises key dates for past events and for the duration of the story. I find keeping timelines in my head extremely challenging, but I have an intense emotional memory, so once I've linked a character's timeline with their emotional changes, I can remember chronology. Also, knowing a character's birthdate or when they first had sex or last lied to someone they loved can be important for your story. The act of writing out timelines deepens a sense of character memory as you revisit key changes in their past. There is nothing worse than getting in a muddle with your timeline, or at least there's nothing worse for me. Having to rework everything in the story to make it fit after changing the order of events would be impossible for me without a reference. You will have your own area of weakness.

The point is to cultivate character notes that are specific to your *own* needs, not anyone else's.

Unconscious drives

New character dimensions constantly arise from the emerging material. Sometimes though, you're avoiding a difficult question. For example, *Why does he hate his father, what happened there?* You might let your character explore in first-person monologue their feelings about a memory or an attitude. You've been resisting this missing beat but know that it is needed to take the story forward.

This need to fill lived gaps for a character is similar to the reason I might use improvisation with actors on an existing play. As the action develops, you need to enrich a particular emotional memory. For example, I remember doing a day of improvisation with two wonderful actors, Ben Whishaw and Trystan Gravelle, to live through the events being asserted and denied in the cruel penultimate scene of Philip Ridley's chilling *Leaves of Glass*. Having experienced the painful subtext to the scene, they could allow the surface to play, the chaos finally engulfing.

Writing is similar for me. It's emotionally lived rather than a forensic analysis. Sometimes you may need to do some rooting around to explore your character's history, but if you know it all consciously at the start, you run the risk of denying your greatest gift as a writer which comes from exposing your shadow self through the act of writing. When you read work that lacks passion and spontancity it's often because the dark side of the self has been repressed through a writing process of conscious construction. The writer is sticking to the rules where they feel most safe.

If there is a contradiction between the public behaviour of your character and their deepest inner drives, this is also true of you, the writer, in ways you may not be conscious of. Of course it is important to keep your characters separate from yourself in order to see their inner conflict. However, you are often writing from your character's point of view and through that, exploring aspects of yourself.

At the crisis point of most storytelling, a character's public mask slips to reveal their private wound – a previously hidden aspect of themselves which they or others are forced to respond to – whether they confront it or choose to ignore it (**Rule 14**). This kind of contradiction lies at the heart of all human growth and at the heart of you. In creating and devouring stories we are exploring our own potential to transform.

Living with your characters, feeling them with you before you write, is not so much about conscious detailed knowledge as about unconscious inner drive.

RULE BREAKER 12

Let your characters surprise you

RULE 13

Make your main character likeable

This seems to me one of the most limiting rules imposed on us by mainstream culture. It is particularly prevalent in TV, but also film. There is even a screenwriting guide called *Save the Cat!* based on the theory that your main character must do something likeable early on.[10] The problem is that the most interesting characters in art or life are often not immediately likeable. Give an obnoxious main character a good deed early on and we may warm to him while it lasts, but so what? This rule implies that most of the audience view themselves as likeable, so they will want to see this reflected in the story. Is this true?

What's not to like?

If you've a character whom you need to make more sympathetic you can make other characters worse than they are or you can endow them with some likeable qualities. If you do this skillfully it is true that most people will feel more drawn to that character. It is also a manipulative and practical 'by numbers' approach that can lead to a bland, predictable character who no one cares about at all.

Some likeable characteristics

- a rare insight
- clowning, wit, playfulness, self-deprecating humour
- empathetic concern
- an aesthetic response to environment – a sense of beauty or spirituality

- an endearing habit or tick
- kindness
- altruism
- courtesy
- a good listener
- another character lets us know what a sweet person that character is

Character likeability can be useful to hook us in, but it wears thin pretty quickly. Why do I say that? Well, it comes down to what *sustains* our engagement with a character and likeability has little to do with that. Is Macbeth likeable? No. He has more in common with some of the despised dictators overthrown in 2011, when I wrote this book. So why do we care what happens to a tyrant and what do we gain from getting inside his terrifying mind?

Empathy rather than sympathy

It's all to do with the neural human process called empathy and storytelling relies upon it. Empathy is an act of imagination, the ability to put ourselves in someone else's shoes *without* necessarily liking their actions. In fact the less we agree with them, the greater the challenge to our imagination. We experience the feelings of characters and we care about what happens to them, not because we like them or because they are just like us, in any narrow sense, but because through the telling of their story, we have come to understand their motivations, their moral conflict.

What sustains our compassion for a character is their struggle with the world and themselves. Many kinds of struggle can evoke our empathy; fighting for a just cause; trying to achieve a dream; taking on an impossible responsibility; trying to hide pain. It is the act of struggle with which we empathise. In art as in life we identify with the human being in jeopardy having the courage to make change.

Courage and honesty are two of the most admirable human qualities and main characters generally possess or gain one or other quality on their journey. Sometimes a story explores their lack of these qualities in some way. One reason that so many stories are about outsiders, underdogs or free spirits who go their own way may be that we empathise with their struggle and that they are more likely to have these rare qualities of courage (to act) and/or honesty (to face themselves). Without these traits there can be no genuine growth in self-knowledge.

Sympathy doesn't have the same staying power. Unless a story is working on a simplistic level, a main character cannot remain universally likeable even to himself. A character may be a universally good archetype, as in a myth or fairy tale, but universally likeable is a tougher call. As soon as a main character takes a significant action, i.e. they make a change, this character will find themselves in conflict with someone who wants to maintain the status quo. Otherwise where's the story? If an extremely 'likeable' character is honestly drawn, they are likely to also suffer from cowardice and self-deception. So you might start off with a likeable character, but as soon as they create drama they become interesting instead which is far more satisfying.

We relate to stories that reflect human complexity. The life of an average person has huge emotional richness. Most of our lives contain tragedy, or at least secret pain. Most of us have some awareness of our own family, friendship or workplace mythologies. If empathy is cheapened to sympathy, to feeling comforted by nice characters and their likeable traits, the depth of our humanity is reduced to the status of a Facebook friend. Our imaginations will be dulled and we will find ourselves only telling stories to one another that are at best banal and at worst patronising.

Expanding boundaries through empathy

The audience-reader can be encouraged to confront their personal hostility to certain complex characters or to challenge their own conflict around these hostile feelings. It is through stories that we explore the more uncomfortable aspects of our inner landscape using both pleasure and pain. Human beings of all ages have a psychological need for a safe outlet through storytelling and play. In recent years there has been a movement to sanitise the stories that UK children can be told. Perhaps this mirrors the infantilization of adults through 'comfort' stories.

Encouraging the boundaries of human empathy beyond what is immediately recognisable imaginatively expands our cultural, ideological and emotional experiences. This was the philosophy behind my own new writing programmes at The Red Room and Soho Theatre, where some work was viewed as daring in subject matter simply because it was international! I find the immature 'I don't like because I don't recognise' mentality hard to grasp given our diverse, complex culture and I have never been aware of this as a barrier for audiences choosing to engage with the unfamiliar. Indeed the reverse is true: I have witnessed curiosity and a desire for growth.

There is a personality type distinguished by a cold, calculated approach to the lives of others, an inability to empathise or feel remorse. As pointed out in a few recent books on the subject, we are living in a world run in part by psychopaths. Capitalism is the rule of competition and profit; as a system it completely disregards human suffering and need. It is not surprising that growing numbers of people come to reflect the qualities valued by the system that controls us.

Macbeth is a well known example of a character whose dictatorship we recognise in the modern world. He is a walking equivocation, psychopathic in behaviour but deeply sensitive to his own feelings. The first time we hear of him he is a war hero who has killed in the most violent way a rebel leader whose head he 'fixed' on the battlements, just as his own head will be held at the end by Macduff. Between these beheadings, Macbeth defends his new power, fuelled by visions of defeat, his fear of losing control propelling him to ruthlessly destroy others. It is the early moments of confusion and remorse that allow us to sense his humanity so our empathy expands to include his paranoiac struggle with himself, not because we approve of him but because we don't. Unless we understand the motivations of a tyrant, how can we confront tyranny in others?

Some writers say that the novel is the most empathic of forms because it relies on the greatest insertion of the reader into the work. The solitary experience of reading enables you to connect with your deepest vulnerability. Others feel that theatre inspires the greatest empathy because you are connecting with living, breathing people and sharing your experience with others in a room. After all, neuroscience tells us that our brainwaves imitate the strongest patterns of those around us.

Whatever the art form, it is your imagination that leads the journey. Empathy comes from imagining your own humanity in another. Writers tend to be more empathetic than most people, simply through imaginative practice, yet they also have a streak of cold detachment, an honest unwavering eye. To justify the fabrication of fiction, your greatest commitment must be to the truth (whatever that means to you). As Philip Ridley puts it 'You have to look at the world through the eyes of an alien, but with a human heart the size of a star.'

Love your cast of characters, including yourself

It is your empathy for your characters that creates compassion in the reader-audience. We've all experienced phoney empathy, where under the guise of compassion someone has tried to manipulate our pain. This can also happen in works of fiction, either because the writer is too calculating and the work tends towards the sentimental, or craft is lacking and the result is clumsy.

Many new writers face the problem of their protagonists not being empathetic enough. This is often to do with self-acceptance (**Rules 12, 14** and **15**). In reality, most writers give themselves to their main character and over-identification can create a kind of unconscious self-censorship. Funnily enough, you may need to create more distance between yourself and your main character in order to fully empathise with them. Change gender, appearance, relationships, anything that you suspect of getting in your way. Ask others to tell you what they think is the most unappealing aspect of your character (or of you). Often they may just say 'I didn't quite believe him,' or 'I wanted to know more from her perspective.' So really explore the inner life of your main character. In allowing them to grow further from you, they express you and you embrace yourself.

You will have heard the truism, 'there are no small parts only small actors.' Anyone who has played a small part may tell you this is wishful thinking. However, if you make your small part in the story as truthful as you can, it will enhance your craft. In this way, writing is the same as acting. E.M. Forster talked about flat and round characters.[11] Generally I think we should try and give all characters a lived truth however undynamic their role in the tale. Dedicating respect and care to your smaller characters enriches your story and your writing process.

RULE BREAKER 13

Expand empathy through your main character's struggle

RULE 14

The antagonist must be big and bad

Writers sometimes long to show how stupid or ineffectual the enemy is. This is tempting, particularly when it seems to reflect a deeper truth. However, weak antagonists can make your work feel authoritarian. Exposing the antagonist's limitations works best once you have shown their disproportionately negative impact. After all, it is their actions which necessitate the reaction of your protagonist, and unless the antagonist seems odds on favourite to win there won't be much of a story.

Of course we're not usually creating one villain – the chair of the board, the serial killer, the Minotaur in his labyrinth. Just as your protagonist may be a whole community, so the antagonist might be the government or even the global capitalist system. There may be (and usually are) various forces of antagonism stacked against your main character. These may be external relationships – public/global or social/domestic. They may be internal obstacles, including your main character's shadow self. At the heart of these conflicts between characters is a moral conflict, a conflict of values.

Obstacles may also be environmental – such as lack of time or a storm or being caught on CCTV. It's true that non-human antagonists are rarely moral opponents but their very inflexibility can be used to heighten a value-driven conflict and often is. All levels of conflict also compete with one another. It's up to you as a writer how you prioritize your main character's conflicts through the progression of the work and how you turn the struggle into your story. Of course your other characters will have conflicts too if they are to be believed.

Broadly speaking, all stories are underdog stories. Some stories add more of a social or political dimension to this, but the nature of storytelling demands it. In Aristotle's time the tragic hero was good because of his noble birth (ha!), but his lack of knowledge gave him a disadvantage. This *hamartia* or 'innocent error' was a force of antagonism often predetermined by the Gods. In the religious, ideological wars of the Renaissance, the guilty and the erring lurked everywhere and the main character lost his innocence, becoming at least partly to blame for his flaw. The most important antagonist in storytelling today is usually the inner self – split between subjective progress and the status quo. Today's reader-audience wants to see this inner-antagonist realised, healed, transformed, destroyed or integrated in some way. If this inner-antagonist is a fighter or a joker, we may even identify with them or enjoy their wit. Certainly we can empathise with their avoidance of pain.

You may choose to design your whole story around the process whereby your protagonist's inner-antagonist transforms (or doesn't). I find the metaphor of the mask can be helpful when thinking about public face/private pain, the projected self distracting from the wound. Think about this in relation to your own main character. How are they getting in their own way? What is their deepest fear? What do they feel would be the worst thing that someone could say about them? Your answers here will expose their wound. The wound is the difficult bit that they are both nursing and trying to hide from the world; the bit they can't fully acknowledge, even to themselves. So, often unconsciously, they don the mask of an opposite or 'easier' quality. Of course wearing the mask is harder work and it can ultimately destroy your character, but they must keep wearing it to control how they are seen. They may be unaware that another option is possible.

So, here are two familiar examples. Someone who fears intimacy might sleep around to ensure it never happens, wear the mask of not believing in love and genuinely believe they haven't met the right person. To fully unmask them another character would need to say and mean 'I love you'. Someone who fears their inner chaos may be very ordered, neat and controlling. To unmask them, a chaotic and emotionally open character might need to be introduced.

In terms of story design, you might allow the mask of the main character to slip a little more in every scene and let us glimpse their wound through their coping strategies. These might include projecting negative emotions onto someone else; rationalizing the trauma; neurotic or passive-aggressive behaviour; believing the opposite of what they feel; denial; displacement; isolation or humour. The trauma that first triggered this psychological mechanism is conventionally revealed about two thirds of the way through the story as the protagonist faces herself (**Rule 9**, pp.70-71). Greater sophistication around psychological issues these days means that audience-readers need less overt explanation.

You might take almost any piece of dialogue, but here is a nice little example of unmasking from *This Isn't Romance* by In-Sook Chappell, fittingly a play about identity. Miss Lee is a translator at an adoption centre in South Korea. Miso, a broke, washed-up ex-model has arrived there from England to find the brother she abandoned when she was adopted as a child. Miss Lee casually unmasks Miso's unbearable guilt about what she did and how long it has taken her to face it. The following exchange happens a few lines into the first scene.

MISS LEE: Is this your first time in Seoul?

MISO: No… I…

MISS LEE: I mean, your first time back?

MISO: Oh…yes.

MISS LEE: How old are you?

MISO glares at her.

MISO: Thirty two, Korean thirty-three.

MISS LEE looks her up and down, looks at her bag.

MISS LEE: Jimmy Choo?

MISO: Err…yes.

MISS LEE: Did your husband?

MISO: No, I don't have a husband.

MISS LEE: No husband, no family.

MISO: No.[12]

Everything Miss Lee says tears at Miso's public mask of being young and successful and returning to Korea to find her family and do the right thing. As we see from this, masks can often seem better, more 'good.' Neither are they necessarily false. As part of the character's aspiration to escape herself the mask expresses incompletion. Miss Lee questions Miso's integrity and credibility by asking some apparently innocent questions and Miso is trapped with her denied self.

Here are just a few of Miso's conflicts in this little extract:

> with Miss Lee
> with authority and older women generally
> between her raw emotion and the formality of the set up
> between her two countries
> her guilt and love for her absent brother
> struggling to control her anger
> wanting to do the right thing and feeling it's too late
> wanting to appear together whilst she's falling apart
> between needing and denying family

Unmaskings tend to lead to sudden and unexpected emotional moments – at the end of this scene, Miso violently turns on Miss

Lee. However, unmaskings also have a gradual cumulative effect and don't need to be acknowledged by a character to register with an audience-reader. Unmaskings show us what challenges the character will need to face in the story. Going into her next scene, Miso strengthens her mask and in our production, the actress instinctively donned her designer shades.

The idea of unmasking may sound mechanical but, if you're having trouble with the turning of a scene, it's worth applying the idea as a metaphor. It might help you to improve the shape and design of the conflict, the intensity, tone and pace and if it doesn't, other solutions may present themselves through the process of exploration.

Thinking about your main character's wound as an inner-antagonist may also help you to find compassion for the darker forces in your story in order to be truthful to them. The most frightening villains have their own vulnerability that we also understand. They are not simply big and bad like cartoon characters, they are as human and richly complex as your protagonist. The external antagonist might express your main character's deepest fears. In this way, fighting the antagonist means your main character must confront herself.

Sometimes, the protagonist in your story is an anti-hero. You might think of this character as an antagonist or as a protagonist who has given in to their baser instincts, their dark side. Sometimes a potential hero becomes an anti-hero through the drama, as in one of my favourite plays, Georg Büchner's *Woyceck* (1836), in which the protagonist is driven mad by his masters, making it the first working-class tragedy, 2000 years on from Aristotle.

If you ever need a quick 'by numbers villain' or you need to make any character seem meaner, you can simply reverse the 'what's not to like' list in **Rule 13**. For example, the trait of appreciating beauty. To reverse this, show a character violating or ignoring something beautiful. I once saw my landlord kick over a music stand with a flute on it, cursing that it was in his path. A tiny moment of violation, but I found it hard to like him after that. It hurts to see beauty or possibility senselessly destroyed.

RULE BREAKER 14

The antagonist is also you

RULE 15

Keep your main character active

One hour later she was dead. So it goes.

Kurt Vonnegut, *Slaughterhouse-Five*

When I was preparing to write this book, I talked to many writers about what they found most challenging, and keeping their main character active topped the list. We all know that main characters are not fixed entities, but dynamic, ever-changing – transforming their world. So what's the key to creating an active character and why can it seem so hard to achieve?

In **Rule 14** we discussed the balance between who your characters believe themselves to be and who they authentically are, between what they say and what they do; between intention and action. Therein lies the key to this rule too. An active character and strong opposition are interdependent. This is because character reveals itself through action taken under pressure. That pressure may be external or internal and, as we saw in the scene between Miss Lee and Miso (pp.105-106), usually one provokes the other.

So the main way to create a more active main character is to intensify the forces acting against her, the unfamiliar obstacles that necessitate choices and actions. By definition the actions she takes will not resolve things until the end. Until then her inner and outer antagonists seem to conspire to ensure that her action has the opposite effect to that intended, opening the gap between expectation and reality, taking her further from her deepest need. She will literally get in her own way. Even when she responds in a positive way to unmasking, showing us a glimpse of an integrated future character, it's never enough.

Progressively this conflict intensifies what's at stake for her changing version of the future. She is forced to take ever more extreme choices/actions to attempt to close that reality gap which mirrors the divided self. With all this to deal with, an active character must also possess the stamina and willfulness to keep resisting. Think of your story as the most significant event in your character's life and you'll want to make it as full and vital as possible.

It's true that most people do as little as necessary to get the result they want and this is a useful benchmark in storytelling, forcing you to up the ante (raise the stakes). However, a wounded character is likely to either overreact or underreact (by other characters' standards), to any given attack. So creating an active main character is about clearly motivated proportionate action, not in any objective sense, but to the specific tolerance of your changing character in their changing world.

If your main character seems too passive, act out his scenes to identify where the plot holes are, where the action sags or the stakes don't rise. Physicalising your story can show you at once where you need to tighten or intensify the main character action. So can telling your character's story in terms of every blow, each major change. Try narrating it from the audience-reader point of view and from different character perspectives.

In your dreams you are the main character and in your story this may be true too. At the end of **Rule 13** we identified this as a challenge to creating an empathetic main character. You take them for granted, putting them through too many or too few problems, particularly when you are unconsciously driven to resolve your own issue through that character. Too much grief and you have a passive victim, too little and you have a passive observer. Your character is crushed or they sail through unscathed. In either case they will seem two dimensional, less real.

For your main character, passivity can also be a positive act of resistance or avoidance. Of course, if you, the *writer*, are passive about expressing this, then it's simply avoidance. Many heroes are reluctant, forced into action against their will. They may never truly commit to action or do so very late in the story such as in Khaled Hosseini's *The Kite Runner* (2003). Sometimes your character makes an internal reflective journey, but this can still be about choice and growth.

I developed and directed for stage and radio Hassan Abdulrazzak's first play, the multi-award-winning *Baghdad Wedding* (2007). The screenplay is now in development with Focus Features. The passive main character, Marwan, is also our narrator. Hassan explains:

> 'If one goes with the assumption that two golden rules of writing are 'avoid flashbacks' and 'keep main character active' then I guess on a surface level, it could appear that in *Baghdad Wedding*, I broke both rules. But I think what happened was an organic solution that inadvertently challenged these two rules simultaneously. Hence, Marwan, arguably the central protagonist of the play, serves a not too dissimilar function to Nick Carraway in *The Great Gatsby*. He is the observer/narrator, commenting on the actions of other, more 'active' characters in the story. His very inaction is highlighted in the end as a choice and has profound consequences for him. However, when it came to adapting the play for the screen, the device of the semi-inactive narrator, that works so well in the intimate and live setting of a theatre stage became cumbersome and artificial. Hence, he is the character that has perhaps undergone the greatest change for the screenplay adaptation'.

One solution to the issue of the passive main character is to split the main character and protagonist functions and I think in the play of *Baghdad Wedding* that's how Hassan gets around the issue. Diffident Marwan is the main character whilst sexy Salim is the active protagonist. Even in the section of the play that we believe Salim to be dead, Marwan's eulogy to his best friend's beautiful wildness and profound influence on his life is constantly usurped by its subject.

> SALIM: ...You were saying I don't give a damn who you sleep with. I accept you as a brother.
>
> MARWAN : We never talked openly about it... Maybe there was no need. I filled in the missing pieces later from your novel.
>
> SALIM: The hug was enough. It was beautiful; said everything. And anyway a few days after, we fucked.
>
> MARWAN: What?! We never did!
>
> SALIM: I know but I am dead now. ...I can say whatever I like.[13]

In the second half of the play, Salim steals the entire narrative from Marwan to tell his own adventure of kidnap and torture which ends with him stealing the woman Marwan loves but didn't fight for. The narrative returns to Marwan at the end of the play when he shares his dream with the audience, a nightmare vision for the future of Iraq, 'a country found and lost again.'

All active except the main character

How do you maintain the centrality of your main protagonist's journey, when you have multiple characters with strong wills, stories and points of view? This is a common challenge for some very talented new writers including Maxine Quintyne-Kolaru who posed this question. In her play *Take Me to Manhattan* she has created a tragi-comic array of vivid, wounded London characters. Her main character is their fragile teenage victim.

- Take those unruly characters to task and don't let them just take over whenever they like. Revel in their wildness but let them serve a story design – shift the balance. Subordinate them to the story of the protagonist or of the community as protagonist.

- Make more of the passive main character's point of view; let us see the grotesque characters only through her eyes. Perhaps let her grow in stature through her gradual separation from or reconciliation with them.

- Ensure that the story of your protagonist is active by making her more wilful. Trace the ups and downs of her journey. Is she in the driving seat enough?

- Don't have a main character. Allow each character their story and point of view which takes precedence in different scenes/chapters yet drives the story forward. *The Slap* by Christos Tsiolkas is a superb example of this in the novel form.

Active versus passive and the creation of subtext

Sometimes characters appear to under-react to events in story terms. Passive responses are strongest when turned into positives or what we term in rehearsal 'playable' actions. The key to this is focusing on what your character wants from an encounter and how they go about trying to get it. Playable actions become clear in a rehearsal room when we 'action' a scene, finding the beat changes.† The action of *how* your character tries to achieve their goal will be a playable transitive verb. In other words, it is directed at someone or something. For example: *she teases him; he begs her; she seduces him; he crushes her.* This tactical, transitive verb only changes when a character wins or loses a beat or changes their mind. Their goal may remain the same throughout a scene, but their *action,* their verb changes – hence unit of action.

Look back at the Miso and Miss Lee scene (pp.105-106). To your mind, is it one beat or two? If there is a change, where is it?

---

† Stanislavski broke scenes into units of action or 'beats' – this was how 'bits' sounded in Stanislavski's strong Russian accent – and we still break scenes into beats today as a way of navigating the emotional journey.

Who is driving the action? What verbs might you choose for the characters' 'hows'? OK this may be about acting but in terms of writing, if you have a scene that just isn't working, it may be helpful to break it down and think about how your character tries to achieve what they consciously want, as well as how this may contradict their unconscious need. This hidden need is called the subtext.

Embrace inaction

Of course, there are many genres and forms which deliberately eschew the notion of active character, using other means to captivate a reader-audience. In some of the non-linear works cited in **Rule 10** you will find passive characters. Beckett's work is full of them. Continuing to exist, to wait, to play, to reflect, his characters' literal inaction becomes a metaphor for the human condition. Fernando Arrabal, in works such as *Guernica,* also creates characters trapped in a world of hateful, terrible confusion. 'Because confusion is what dictators find most unbearable!' he proclaimed when I heard him speak in Dublin in 2010. Another anti-war work, Kurt Vonnegut's *Slaughterhouse-Five* has Dresden survivor Billy Pilgrim thrown around by time travel and surrendering free will. So it goes.

You may need a lot of self-knowledge to write stories that seem true to others. Creating a clear, active protagonist is part of that journey, but it may require even greater self-knowledge to deliberately create a passive main character. Passive main characters are harder to sustain but for some writers, psychologically and/or politically, this might feel like the only honest way to express the absurdity of our barbarous world.

RULE BREAKER 15

Show the human condition through character inaction

RULE 16

Your characters must be distinct from one another

This is one of those rules which appears obvious but it's also a bit misleading. Yes, your characters are all particular people so they need to look, sound and behave differently from each other and from you. There is a danger that your voice can overwhelm them; over-control them to the point where they don't seem to have any independent existence. However, your characters will always share the distinctiveness of their creator. They are part of your world. You bring them to life, you also live through them.

Character function, needs, characteristics and voice

In early drama, when the Muse took the rap and credit for your work, the archetype was a mask. Replicating or mistaking character function was pretty impossible. In modern psychological writing, deep character is what's *behind* the mask, as discussed in previous rules. It is also an aspect of you, the writer, and the boundaries between you and your characters can become unintentionally blurred. You suddenly discover that you've created two characters with a dying parent or abandonment issues or a love of romantic poetry. They aren't relevant to your fictional story, but they are to your personal narrative.

Such similarities can only work if they contribute to your overall design and are used for thematic effect. Random repetition feels sloppy unless it's a deliberate strategy, as in Caryl Churchill's brilliant *Blue Kettle*, which weaves these two words into the meaning of her play like faulty DNA or a language virus spreading absence and destruction.

In prose fiction, repetitions of quite surface characteristics can trip you up unexpectedly. For example, you realise that two new characters on a page have names that sound similar to an existing character or perhaps both their names begin with the letter B. You notice that you have unconsciously imposed your own stylistic tics on all your characters. They never smile, they always grin; all are defined by their relationship to colour and none seem to have a sense of smell.

Character functions often repeat. Sometimes a few minor functionaries can be amalgamated into one full-bodied character. One test of whether or not a character is minor is how easily you can replace them. Is the young girl in scene three carrying out the same story function as the old man in scene seven? Merging minor characters can immediately strengthen a story and sometimes it's necessary to do this with more major characters to avoid dilution of function. Orchestrating the right amount of characters and casting the story you need to tell, is best done fairly early on or you can face intricate and messy rewrites. Of course sometimes you don't know which characters you can discard until later in the process.

Character-combining happens a lot in theatre, often for reasons of financial rather than artistic economy, since most budgets are based on small cast sizes. Excepting a handful of national companies, a Shakespearean sweep is rarely permitted for playwrights today, making films and novels more appealing to epic writers.

To check how the overall composition is working, track the storylines of your characters and see what is dispensable. You might also do an entrances/exits chart, a simple graph to show you at a glance how much 'stage-time' the character has, which characters are together and when. Nowadays, writing software can do this for you.

Your characters all want different things and therefore react differently to the same situation through their use of language and the way they communicate with one another. Creating believable dialogue is discussed in **Rule 18**. However, the notion of an 'ear for dialogue' is *not* about an ability to mimic real speech. It is an ability to create characters who believably speak the way they do. Once your character lives, as long as you actively listen and loosen your control, then you will hear their voice clearly.

Even when your characters are based on real people or observations, it is your imagination that allows them to belong in your world. Booker Prize-winning novelist Howard Jacobson says:

> 'If you write what you've overheard, it will sound like something that you've overheard. It has to go; it has to pass through you first. It has to have the permission. A character has to have the permission of your soul before it becomes a character. A character isn't vivid by virtue of your having seen a vivid person in life. Nothing lives, nothing in a novel lives, neither character nor story nor anything else until it is written. By which I mean until it has become yours.'[14]

Having a distinct voice as a writer is an advantage. If your characters are living, breathing individuals, then they will also be distinct and you don't need to worry about that aspect too much. If they are not alive in your mind when you write them, they probably won't live in the reader's either.

RULE BREAKER 16

Your characters all belong to you

RULE 17

Put off writing dialogue for as long
as possible

This rule concerns dialogue in drama. Philosophically, the idea of delaying writing dialogue for as long as you can, feels connected to **Rule 12, Know as much detail as possible about your characters**. The more complete the world you create in your mind, the more likely you are to capture something of it on the page; it will be less of a pale imitation.

Putting off writing dialogue is not necessarily bad advice to new writers. It is a rule aimed at remedying speech that sounds flat and wooden because the writer has launched into dialogue without hearing or feeling his characters. Or it could be that their voices sound authentic but the writer doesn't have the skill or imagination to give them clear wants for their scene; their reason for being together could bring their exchanges to life.

Playwright Roy Williams uses a clever exercise to hold back the force and energy of character desire until the dialogue is literally bursting to come out. It is an original and practical take on this rule and can also be used to overcome writer's block.

> 'Take out two characters, whatever play you are writing, place them in a simple setting, like a bus stop for example. Spend the next few pages with them only talking about when the bus is going to arrive and nothing else! Make it as boring as possible, no characterization, no energy, no life, anything! Believe me, it is not as easy as it sounds. A soon as you feel like making the scene more interesting,

start writing it! It is also useful to suss out a real writer from a false one. A real writer's words would have started to kick in, probably by page three, a false writer will be having his or her characters still talking about the bus by the time they get to page thirty!'

Dialogue drives the story

Seasoned dramatists know instinctively when they are ready to start writing. For playwright Paul Sirett, best known for hit musical *The Big Life* (2004), dialogue is the central driver of the whole creative process.

> 'I totally disagree with this rule. I always start with writing dialogue. For me, the most creative aspect of writing is writing dialogue. I use writing dialogue to solve problems. If I don't know what's happening in a story, I write dialogue to find out. If I have planned a scenario and the dialogue takes me somewhere else I trust the dialogue.'

The more alive and fresh you are in the actual moment of writing, the more your unconscious creative impulse takes over. You've just got to get it down on paper quickly enough. That's easier when there's no mental clutter or laborious joining of dots. When the characters start talking, you start writing and that's when you'll really get to know them and where they want to go. You don't know what your characters will say but if they rebel against your preconceived scenario you can be pretty sure they're for real!

RULE BREAKER 17

Use dialogue to discover the story

RULE 18

Create believable dialogue

Here is another rule that sets out to remedy dialogue lacking subtext or speakability or any sense that it was once in a human mouth. Actors do wonders to breathe life into dead drama, but on the page, inert, clumsy speech takes your reader straight out of the story.

Living dialogue happens when you're writing from your character's point of view in their authentic time/place. Making your dialogue believable is to hear/see/inhabit your characters talking and to write down what's happening. Let them surprise you. Read your dialogue aloud or better still ask someone to read it for you; your ear is sharper than your eye when it comes to words on the page.

When we talk about 'believable,' of course, that means artistically – not in reference to real life, but the life of the work, the world you've made up. In Caryl Churchill's previously mentioned play, *Blue Kettle*, the believable world is one where by the end the characters are talking in syllables and consonants from the words 'blue' and 'kettle' where everything else has gone. Aware of the artifice we still believe in its integrity to itself. After all even so-called realistic dialogue is a construction. The style or tone of dialogue, the use of language, is always specific to what you're writing. Realistic dialogue often refers to recognisable features of real speech in the dialogue, some of them mentioned below.

In theatre, there are certain amusing clichés of dialogue that are all too easy to parody. Perhaps influenced by film, the Royal Court led the fashion for ping-pong dialogue, or what one writer I know calls the tap dancing school of playwriting. Terse, conflictive exchanges with a semblance of wit or surface shimmer, which hint at a deeper meaning that often eludes. Such thin plays will date quickly.

Tips for rewriting stilted dialogue

I offer these tips in support of rewriting and polishing or as excercises in craft, not as a place to start writing from. Dialogue comes from/defines character desire whereas these are conscious quick fixes.

- Is there any exposition pretending to be people talking? Cut to what you really need for your story and integrate it with the action of the scene. If dialogue meanders, challenge yourself to write your whole scene in approximately half the words. This exercise in economy can help you locate the story movement.

- To ensure that character voices are distinct (**Rule 16**), you can try that old trick of covering up the names to see if you can still tell who is speaking.

- Let the audience know what the character is feeling without them voicing it. In other words, ensure there is subtext. In drama, an actor will always create subtext, whether you give it to them or not. So give them the story you *want* them to tell.

- Is there an unmasking — one character holding up a mirror of truth to the other, perhaps unintentionally? (**Rule 14**)

- If you're a novelist who struggles with dialogue, read drama for inspiration.

- Cut out every description or explanation of emotion that can be shown through dialogue, subtext or action. If you have to tell your reader that your character said it tactfully, in shock, or with anger, or that he chortled, suggested or sulked, then you may be laying it on with a trowel or the dialogue isn't doing its job. You're at risk of creating an awkward tension between dialogue and description which can be disconcerting to read. Like any style question this can only be looked at concretely in context.

- If dialogue falls into a monotonous beat, try disrupting rhythm and pace; make elisions, breaks, allow characters to speak in fragments. Dialogue is an artifice, but these strategies mimic aspects of real speech and can help you create a kind of poetry.
- Create leitmotifs in dialogue, the recurrent images, tics, phrases that accumulate, deepen or even transform in meaning, sometimes to become their opposite.
- Enable gaps and pauses. Use the significance of silence for one or all characters. Think of silence as building to a climax. When speech erupts it will gain in power.
- People often respond indirectly, particularly in informal situations. Let characters give tangential responses or delay the answers rather than answer the question asked. It raises questions for your reader-audience, creating suspense and subtext.
- Consider place and appropriateness. Explore social or personal restrictions on what a character feels able to say and how context changes the way they speak.
- A conversation is interrupted and then resumed. What has changed?
- Build scenes in which one or all of the characters find it really hard to talk. This might be about taboos, emotional limitations or limited vocabulary as in a foreign language or an unfamiliar situation. Their struggle to communicate can be fascinating to watch.
- In prose fiction, keep speaker attributions to a minimum, even if it is simply 'said' and insert at the first natural break in the speech.

Of course all dialogue can be viewed as a construction and tips above ignored for good artistic reason. Which brings me to monologue, the place where theatre was born.

Monologue is a conversation

I adore poetic monologues and have developed and directed many one-person plays that audiences fell in love with too. I think of a one-person play as an action upon the audience who take a role as another character or characters. I've been lucky to have worked with a few awesome monologists – including Kay Adshead, Philip Ridley, Judy Upton and Rob Young. Philip Ridley's characters have a tendency to erupt into extraordinary monologues in the middle of a dialogic scene. In *Piranha Heights* one such two-page monologue was delivered by the wonderful actress Jade Williams in full burka and niqab, only her eyes visible – surely a first on the UK stage. I asked Phil about his distinctive monologues.

'My first play, *The Pitchfork Disney*, is full of monologues. This proved to be a bit of a problem when I was first trying to get the play on. Everyone seemed of the opinion that long speeches held the action up. The audience will get bored, I was told. I was advised to either cut the monologues out altogether or, if I wanted to keep them, break them up, have the other actors throw in little comments, keep the 'ping-pong' backwards and forwards going at all times. I've always felt the monologues were the action. And that far from excluding the other actors on stage, it actually gave them a hell of a lot to do – receiving a story is not a passive experience. It is a dramatic act in itself. After all, it is the core of all Greek tragedy. Someone steps on stage and tells you, in great detail, what has happened off stage. It's spellbinding. What we don't see haunts us far more than what we do. We remember most what our imagination creates for itself. Monologues can be doorways into another person's mind. They can be reportage, crossword puzzle and poem all in one. Monologues are emotional brain scans of a character.

I usually write my monologues in the present tense. I love that feeling of the actor being in the moment, re-living all the things they are describing, creating everything around them with words, feeling everything for the first time. A lot of that 'feeling' is about images. Sometimes an image becomes so potent, has barnacled so much emotional weight through the course of the play, that it suddenly bursts out as a sort of 'image aria'. It sings out and echoes through the auditorium. This usually happens in a monologue. A character suddenly pulls together images that have been seeded before and re-weaves them into one speech that blossoms into a cadenza. The speech has echoes bigger than itself. Lots of musical references, I know. But it does feel like music to me.'

RULE BREAKER 18

Don't confuse realism with truth

RULE 19

'Use regional dialect, patois, sparingly'

Elmore Leonard, *10 Rules of Writing*

This rule at first glance seems to be almost the opposite of **Rule 18**, but it is a received wisdom most often aimed at novelists and screenwriters. The notion is that odd spelling and unknown words pull you from the dialogue into considering its form. In the case of TV, it is said to make life more confusing for the actor if the words are spelt phonetically. The writer of dialogue is accused of trickery, a substitute for true inventiveness.

So how do you convey the unique language of your character(s) and still keep your readers with you? According to this rule, choice of words, syntax, rhythm and grammar are ample tools to have at your disposal.

I disagree. To me there is something magical about being propelled into a new language as part of a new world. Why should we have to standardise language and what is the implication of that? It seems to be the literary equivalent of RP (Received Pronunciation) which theatre has largely abandoned, though it still holds sway in radio drama. Hattie Naylor has won awards for her radio plays and is a firm believer in relishing dialects.

> 'Complete the war against RP on radio – it's a political thing, as the RP accent is the accent of power and authority, giving any individual with such a voice more say in the world. I recently dramatized *Solaris* for radio and was heavily criticized for using the very gifted

actress Joanne Froggatt as the romantic lead – she has a northern accent – implying that for many, the idealized woman comes complete with RP accent – this is truly depressing. If there is anything unclear then either repeat or have someone in the play – i.e. a narrator repeat it for you.'

Some people say writing in dialect is lazy, I might suggest that a reader-audience who can't be bothered to read or listen to dialect is lazy. Is there any middle ground here?

Novelist Anthony Cartwright's characters speak in broad Black Country accents. He shows this on the page, partly phonetically, partly through word order and phrasing.

In this conversation from his novel *Heartland* (2009), one of the central characters, Rob, an ex-professional footballer, is in conversation with a boy he coaches.

Footballers shunt smoke.
I ay a footballer.
Yer was a footballer.
Was is different.

Anthony explains his choices:

'Generally in publishing anything 'regional' is seen as a bit suspect… I think Leonard's ten rules are good ones, but I had to find a way to represent the way my characters talk realistically – I wanted to try and find a way of getting the sound of Dudley into the reader's head. I didn't think this was going to happen by using standard English, even with altered syntax, so I went for it fairly unsparingly. Doing what I've done also allows different characters to sound different, and for their accents to come and go, depending on the situation and who they are talking to, again a feature of real speech. I think I took this approach fully aware of the pitfalls: it's down to me to make this work and not alienate readers. A further outcome of taking this approach, incidentally, was my abandonment of speech marks. Avoid stylistic affectations is usually another useful general writing rule, or 'no tricks' as Raymond Carver puts it, so again, messing about with conventional punctuation is a bit of a risk. I did it to blur some of the lines between speech and thought, standard English and dialect.'

I think James Kelman's *A Chancer* (1985) was the first novel I read to take a similar approach. In theatre we've tended to relish breaking this particular rule to the point where by convention we play quite freely with it. Rule-breaking examples that inspired me were Amani Naphtali's *Ragamuffin* (1990), Irvine Welsh's *Trainspotting* (novel 1993 swiftly followed by stage adaptation) and Enda Walsh's *Disco Pigs* (1996). In theatre *everything* is in speech marks. I wonder if this has a similar leveling effect to Anthony abandoning them in his novel.

Many plays I've developed and directed have broken this rule to some degree. A recent one was *Shraddhā* (2009) at Soho Theatre (Meyer-Whitworth Award 2010) for which Natasha Langridge created a new poetic language based on Romany cadences and words. Here, Pearl, a London Romany teenager sounds off about the clearing of their site to make way for the Olympics. Her nephew was almost run over.

PEARL
That close it was.
Like being in starry all of us can't even let the chavvies play out case
they get run down by bleedin tractor
The races 'aven't started yet you know

The main issue we needed to consider was authenticity and potential offence (**Rule 29**). Natasha isn't Romany and although she had spent a number of years researching her play with Romanies, understandably there are cultural sensitivities. The way I got around this was to have a Romany assistant director and a dialect coach who could both ensure that the poetic language sounded like a Romany-based poetry in the mouths of the actors. The test of this was the day that we had a Romany panel discussion and a large Romany audience. One woman said to me she thought that the actors were Romany and was shocked to hear their real voices.

RULE BREAKER 19

Delight in distinctiveness

RULE 20

Keep 'em guessing

A man's power is in the half-light, in the half-seen movements of his hand and the unguessed-at expression of his face. It is the absence of facts that frightens people: the gap you open, into which they pour their fears, fantasies, desires.

Hilary Mantel, *Wolf Hall*

We live in an impatient age; an age of creating false needs that keep us in a permanent state of want. Story is driven by expectation, the desire to know what will happen next, but if you reward impatience and give it to people straight, then there's no mental or emotional striving, no need to listen further. In life, people who withhold information can be maddening, but in fiction we enjoy the mental puzzle of trying to work them out.

This principle works at a primal emotional level. The unconscious doesn't know the difference between reality and fiction, so the feelings of fear, pleasure and compassion aroused in the reader-audience are real. Deferring gratification is an art. A good storyteller knows instinctively when to hold back information and when to release it, when to conceal and reveal. If you show too much too early, you limit the imaginative scope of your reader-audience who is glued for clues and generally more sophisticated than you think.

Ways to keep 'em guessing

Some of the following can be approached as exercises but mostly they are just techniques to consider in relation to your own and other's work.

- Imply a question for the audience-reader, then delay the answer for as long as you can keep them working for it. Creating mystery is different to creating confusion, which is best avoided, unless you're sure of what you're doing (**Rule 22**).

- Using misdirection is another staple of storytelling – make us think the story is going one way, when in fact it's going another. While you're at it, use your diversionary tactic to deepen the main story or theme or create a subplot. A favourite use of misdirection is to give your characters false expectations – allow them to envisage a future. We'll suspect dramatic irony, so you're letting us think we're a step ahead. Now twist it. Don't give us the opposite future we're expecting. Connect with another thread and *really* surprise us.

- High stakes and deep conflict increase jeopardy and therefore tension. Keep us fearing for what your character may lose and hoping for what they might gain whilst putting them at increasingly high risk – invite us to go through their struggles under duress, face their dangerous situation. The conflict between fear and hope in us creates suspense about whether the character will be destroyed or saved. Ensure that what's at stake for your character becomes important for the audience-reader too through empathy. 'Oh no, they're going to lose/I'm going to lose'. Prolong the apprehension.

- If a character's unaware of the danger they're in, we'll feel even greater concern/suspense. We want to warn them and we can't, which provokes a strong physical feeling of anxiety and frustration. Only in pantomime do we shout 'Behind you!' and by convention the warning is unheeded, because it would kill the suspense. Though we know it is to no avail, still we shout.

- Another version of this is the 'loaded gun' described by Chekhov. If a gun goes off in act three, he said, make sure we see it in act one. Usually, the explosion we're waiting for is emotional rather than literal. One of my favourite pay off examples is at the end of *Brighton Rock*, Graham Greene's terrifying portrait of a young psychopath. I'm thinking of that final moment when Rose goes home to play the cruel recording Pinkie made for her earlier in the book. Greene has used point of view to make us complicit in the foreshadowing of 'the worst horror of all'.

- On the subject of point of view, there are challenges to creating suspense in first person narrative – the danger of the reader-audience feeling overly 'played' since the narrator already knows what happened. However, there can be a suspense-filled and pleasurable aspect to this. I think the solution is to approach it like any other kind of storytelling, using the techniques outlined in this section, but meshed with a sense of self-discovery in the process of telling, allowing us to live through the story moment to moment. The character withholds information for good emotional reason and grows emotionally with the process of telling, as one might through a process of therapy. Lionel Shriver's *We Need To Talk About Kevin* is a superb example of this, subverting an old-fashioned genre, the epistolary novel, and keeping us guessing as to why it is monologic until the very end.

- Mini cliffhanger. Same principle as **Rule 11**, but at the *end* of the scene/chapter/beat. Like a cool party guest, arrive late and leave early – no draining the dregs in the kitchen at the end. The moment you've provoked curiosity, cut to something else and 'hit the ground running' at an even deeper level of the dilemma. It heightens an audience-reader's hunger to know.

- Classic suspense has a slow build, then a sharp increase of pace. Shorter sentences with shorter words is an obvious way to increase pace (reverse this for slowing pace). Related to this, frequently changing the image, beat, paragraph or scene sharpens the time between new sensations and can increase the tension. You might also intensify the action and emotion and/or cut description or physical action. These tempo techniques can be applied to any act of storytelling, including directing. Remember too that pace is just a tool and you need to vary your use of tempo to create intrigue, else a story can become boringly frenetic. Don't confuse suspense with speed.

- Few new playwrights consider the challenge of creating transitions that entertain, take no time or both. A writer has a character moving from a realistically detailed bedroom, for example, to winter forest in falling snow with a rhythm that implies a three-second cross-fade. Perhaps in their imaginations, their play is a film or on a revolve at the National Theatre. I have secretly grown to love such challenges as a director, but transitions in all mediums are a challenge for the writer. Consider how you are keeping us hooked in.

- Suspend time by expanding into magical time. Hypnotise us with your wondrous visions, underscore with music or soundscape, take us back to a childlike state of enchantment, pleasure or horror. In a state of flow, we are absorbed and lose all sense of time.

- Another way to intensify suspense is to put the clock on your story, create a 'race against time' and give your antagonist the advantage. This can be subtly done. Make a list of occasions in your own life when time was an antagonist.

- Tantalise your reader-audience by putting your characters in a situation where they need to conceal their feelings or their deepest needs from one another. Relish the hesitation, the unbearable tension.

- Release information about a character very slowly. You can take us right up to the crisis point before we really get to see them and what the stakes are. The confessional reveal at this classic point is less important, but it's worth trying out how far **Keep 'em guessing** can work through character.

- If something terrible happens early on to someone close to your main character, we feel the risk to them increase too. The main character therefore gains in story stature.

- Create a feeling of uncertainty or unease around a particular place, character or memory moment. The antagonist is somehow lurking.

- Subverting expectation is the key to storytelling and keeping us hooked. But what about shocks? By their 'out of the blueness', shock moments tend to lack suspense and can jolt us out of the fiction. When shock is over-used we feel conned. A technical tip to making shocks work is earlier misdirection and withholding key information so that the shock genuinely turns our world upside down but doesn't seem coincidental. Used very sparingly and with emotional depth, a shock can pull us further into your world and force us to look at the real world in a new way. Think of the unseen baby being stoned to death in *Saved* or the young boy's screams as he is butchered offstage in *Mercury Fur*. These shocks are visceral and unbearable, suspense turns into trauma, an experience so emotionally devastating that we are compelled to stay with it because we want to make it stop. The greatest shocks are rarely what we see; they are what we imagine and how we feel about ourselves when we do nothing to end the horror. Though critics still called it shocking, in *The Censor*, Anthony Neilson subverts what might have been a shockster moment in a lesser play – a woman defecating to arouse a man sexually – and he turns it into a beautiful moment between potential lovers, complete with birdsong. When I saw the play in Istanbul a few years later, this moment was performed off stage. Try listing the strongest shocks you have experienced in fictional worlds, then go back and work out how the writer achieved an impact.

- Use visual and verbal foreshadowing. This plays on our belief that everything exists for a reason in a story, so we have a heightened awareness of signs, symbols and metaphors. The style and tone of the story will indicate how much significance to attach to them.

What keeps 'em guessing more?

Rachel Anthony explains how she wanted to build suspense in a more organic way than the soap she was writing for would permit. Her experience reminds us that there are many different ways to achieve a desired emotional effect.

'When I was working at *EastEnders*, at one point there was a rule that a scene couldn't go on for more than three pages without cutting away to another scene. I had a scene that was about five or six pages long, I think it was Grant and Tiffany in the Vic – and I felt that cutting away and then cutting back to them would break the tension building up. Before I ever worked on *EastEnders* I'd seen a fantastic Tony Jordan episode, where Phil and Sharon had been having an affair and were arguing upstairs at the Vic while Grant was downstairs, and I was almost shouting at the screen for them to keep their voices down – it was a brilliant scene and the tension was sustained by staying with them. Luckily I had Kath Mattock as my script editor and she agreed with me and we argued to keep my scene complete rather than inserting some other random scene halfway through it. Then when Kath went to meet Tony Garnett at World Productions, to talk about working on *The Cops*, she talked to him about our battle to stay with the characters rather than cutting away – and later, when she'd got the job, she found that this was part of the mission statement of *The Cops*, that they wouldn't use artificial cutaways to impose a false pace or tension – they wanted it to feel more like real life, where tension builds where you are. Then I worked at World for about four years, on a few different shows, and they were wonderfully innovative, and made so many inspiring and groundbreaking shows because they always looked for a new angle on drama, and challenged conventions.'

Do we need to keep 'em guessing?

No, these are techniques which you may use, play with, break, expose. There are no rules about what you do. Suspense is a conventional storytelling strategy. Personally I find it fascinating. The mechanisms and devices outlined above are not simply cheap tricks though they may be employed in that way. Like the storytelling to which it contributes, I think suspense takes its prompt from something deep in the psyche – for example our sense of incompletion, our impossible desire to be whole, our need to survive and, of course, our compassion for others. Dreams seem to be almost entirely suspenseful, at least in my experience, but I don't know if that's true for everyone.

There are many kinds of writing that are not constructed around suspense. They tend to be non-linear, poetic, narrative or episodic. Suspense taps in to primal feelings and work without suspense may be more meditative, reflective, cerebral, self-referential, distancing. Work which eschews plot suspense may nonetheless employ suspenseful sequences. You only need to think of Eisenstein's montage technique combined with a suspenseful sequence such as the pram rolling down the Odessa Steps in *The Battleship Potemkin.*

Non-suspenseful work that has influenced me includes interactive or deconstructive theatre (e.g. Augusto Boal's Forum, Living Theatre, Ontroerend Goed), postmodern novelists (e.g. Vonnegut, Acker, Cortázar) and many German playwrights (e.g. Brecht, Handke, Müller). How about you?

The playwright Bertolt Brecht wasn't a fan of **Keep 'em guessing**. He preferred to tell an audience the end at the beginning, to create ironic disruptions to our expectations through political narrative rather than suspense. He wanted to keep us curious about the process of social relationships rather than being focused on the end result. In another kind of play *Mother Courage* would have been a sentimentalized woman, serving the war effort. But in Brecht's play she is neither motherly nor courageous, she is a cowardly monster who is part of the war machine, profiting from the misery that finally swallows all her family and still the horror doesn't stop her.

For Brecht, this forensic dissection, this lack of suspenseful experience was a political act. He didn't want the emotional immersion necessary for suspense, he wanted us to experience the 'means of production' from theatre lanterns to story mechanics or character construction, in the hope that we would see what is extraordinary in what we take for granted, what injustice has been normalised. But Brecht was not entirely pure of suspense. He relishes those climactic sequences at the end of *Mother Courage.* It is pretty hard to completely ignore suspense when you're telling a story, however episodic or montage-based.

Augusto Boal took the Brechtian idea further with forum theatre, initially a 'rehearsal for revolution' that enabled the audience to take control of the narrative. In forum as in many other kinds of interactive performance, suspense cannot be manipulated in the same way, but the possibility of surprise or shock through real-life random occurrences rather than foreshadowing, creates a tension of anticipation.

Kurt Vonnegut said in his advice to short story writers:

> 'Give your readers as much information as possible as soon as possible. To hell with suspense. Readers should have such complete understanding of what is going on, where and why, that they could finish the story themselves, should cockroaches eat the last few pages.'[15]

In *Slaughterhouse-Five* (1969) Kurt Vonnegut gives us the beginning, end and climax pretty much upfront. His struggle to write a novel dealing with his youthful experience of the Dresden bombing frames the flat character life of Billy Pilgrim who has come 'unstuck in time'. Again Vonnegut's decision not to 'traffick' his traumatic experience of Dresden with traditional 'glamourising' techniques of thrills and suspense and rounded characters leads to an astonishing rule-breaking novel.

It is intriguing to consider how little suspense you need to retain the interest of your reader-audience. I know what holds my attention is less about the **Keep 'em guessing** of plot and more about psychological curiosity or just the emotional experience.

Children love to hear the same story told repeatedly, even when they know what's coming because they want to relive the emotion – the hope, the fear. Adults cry at the movie they've seen five times before. As a director in rehearsal, I still feel for the characters in danger when I've watched the same scene repeatedly, when I've engineered the emotional response or even written it myself! Why does it make me laugh or move me to tears? Why do we still experience foreboding even when we know that the story ends happily?

I suspect that emotional engagement rather than anticipation is the aspect of suspense most vital to holding our attention.

Compassion before curiosity. **Keep 'em caring** more than **Keep 'em guessing**. This has implications for other rules too and the way that as writers we may satisfy our audience-reader.

RULE BREAKER 20

Keep 'em caring

RULE 21

The ending must resolve

The promise of a story is that when we reach the end, we will understand what has changed, how and why. Our main character achieves their goal or they don't – the new world or the status quo triumphs. Aristotle proposed that great works are tragic whilst modern producers prefer the happy end. Either way there is an assumption that for a story to sell well it must fully resolve. The greatest resolved endings are not necessarily about concord but more often contradiction – two meanings compete and the dilemma is resolved/problematised at a satisfying new level of resonance. A bittersweet ending may see the main character achieve their original goal only to realise, for example, that it's no longer what they need or the loss in achieving it was too great.

When I was programming Soho Theatre, I observed this desire in an audience for clear moral resolution. Regardless of darkness, levity, quality or complexity, the greatest determinant of critical and box office success seemed to be the nature of the ending. Plays with endings that intentionally divided theatre audiences were by definition less popular. As were open endings – those which were either morally ambiguous or morally unresolved. On the other hand, Live Art audiences had no issue with moral ambiguity or abrupt endings – they expected novelty and challenge. Even attacking the audience was acceptable. Audiences didn't come to Live Art looking for story satisfaction, but that's what they expected from a play.

So are we conditioned to expect moral satisfaction from stories, even if immorality triumphs or the ending is unhappy? Of course morality shifts with the zeitgeist and the individual audience-reader. The triumph of injustice may be a satisfyingly moral ending, in certain contexts, whilst in others it may feel immoral. There are many exceptions to this moral resolution rule. A technical TV example is the continuing drama series, where the story creates a cliffhanger end at the crisis point but the episode remains a moral comforter.

To achieve a classic resolution

Aristotle said that a good ending feels at once inevitable and surprising. It takes us where we need to go on the basis of where we have been during the beginning and middle of the story, but it does so in an unexpected way. Creating this wonderment can be achieved by amplifying some of the storytelling tools discussed throughout this book. Examples include misdirection, a major reversal, last-minute revelation or new interpretation.

- The whole story leads us away from its first question but for maximum surprise impact misdirect your audience between crisis and climax. Allow them to believe that your protagonist retreated or sold out or will do the opposite of what we want them to. This will increase the suspense and pleasure of the climax.

- If you want your audience to believe that the end is inevitable, the scale and style of the climax should feel consistent with what came before it. Track backwards from your climax looking at how the main story leads to that change. Have you foregrounded the right story elements for your climax? Are there any missing beats?

- Give the climax a strong memory moment (sensory or emotional). Pace and momentum generally gather towards the climax and there is often an explosion of visual or verbal fireworks. At this emotional peak, the main character is usually transformed (not always for the better), and the question posed by the first disruption to the status quo is answered. The stakes need to resonate for the audience-reader as primal. Life/death or freedom/enslavement may not be literal struggles/outcomes but metaphorical or existential. The climax is generally about action but sometimes revelation too.

- Echo the beginning in the end, (or vice versa in terms of your writing process), to signify a satisfying transformation. Use repetition of images, lines of dialogue, metaphors, actions in a new changed world, to enable resonance and deep reflection upon the journey's end. Some works literally end in the same place they began.
- The resolution can be a wrap up, a coda, or a final emotionally satisfying action. It can be healing or devastating – reward or punishment. Or, in some of the greatest endings of all it can be both.

Favourite endings

Read/watch endings of films/plays/books you couldn't forget. Try to identify why they haunt you and what this tells you about the kind of ending you probably aspire to create. My own list would include *Stitching* by Anthony Neilson (theatre), which brings together an extreme of happiness and horror through the audience's knowledge of what will happen to the dancing couple now in love and laughing; *Never Let Me Go* (novel) by Kazuo Ishiguro, combines the extremes of humanity and inhumanity. The search for truth takes Kathy H from her pre-determined path as an obedient clone to experience the deepest human grief, love and desire. At the end she accepts her cruel, absurd fate, hoping the memories of her innocent childhood will see her through the gruesome process of being slowly murdered too. In *Dancer in the Dark* by Lars von Trier (film), the extremes of human hope and horror clash as innocent, blind Selma sings at the gallows. Being hanged prevents her from finishing the song.

Whilst Aristotle's belief that all great plays end in misfortune may coincide with my personal taste, it is certainly not a widely held view today. However, his observation that what motivates the end should be either probable or necessary in story terms, has stood the test of time and fashion.

Think of your own favourite endings; how else might the writers have ended the stories and why would this have felt less satisfying?

Unsatisfying endings

There are no rules, but conventionally, if endings don't feel earned in any way they can feel unsatisfying. Examples are *deus ex machina* (the sudden intervention of the Gods or equivalent); it was all a dream; killing everyone off; winner taking all. It should be pointed out that stories with such unearned, easy endings have sometimes been very successful, particularly with comedy where different 'rules' apply.

Sometimes you resolve your ending in story terms, but bring too many threads together at once. It can feel as if the work doesn't know how to end, either because there are one or more false endings or because several endings compete for our attention at once. Try placing and pacing the resolution of each subplot. That's not to say one big ending can't work, and a false ending before a final twist can be a brilliant device, but it helps to be aware of the issues, particularly if you're juggling multiple storylines.

The ending can't resolve

In any medium great writing has an ability to surprise us and to make us feel that by the end we understand the world a little better than we did at the beginning. Sometimes we are encouraged to rediscover the story again with the benefit of hindsight. *Never Let Me Go*, mentioned above, sent me straight back to the beginning. Sometimes a writer offers optional endings or undermines one ending with another. Sometimes part or all of the resolution is left undecided because it would not be truthful to do otherwise.

Ronan Bennett's brilliant *Top Boy* disturbs its TV audience by giving them moral light at the resolution but denying them moral comfort. We're left in no doubt as to the writer's perspective, but the world he shows us does not reassure us that anything has got better, despite all the characters' best attempts to improve their lives. At the end of Kay Adshead's play, *The Bogus Woman*, the central character is deported and her death is reported matter-of-factly, a shock in itself and a clear resolution, but the date given is tomorrow – it could still be prevented, intensifying our need to act. In both of these works the dilemma remains with us after the resolution.

One of my favourite films, Truffaut's *400 Blows* ends with us sharing the young hero's transcendent flight for freedom from reform school, until the boy has nowhere left to run except into the vast beautiful sea. Now he is trapped by what life is. This moment of freedom and entrapment is summed up in the final freeze-frame when he turns to look back at the unjust world. Rather than feeling frustrated by the lack of resolution, we feel devastated by an image of impossible possibility.

RULE BREAKER 21

Leave the ending up to the audience-reader

Rules 22 - 26

Conventions of style, consistency and economy

Your writing might be 90% crap and 10% genius. The art is knowing which is which. Rules can help you here, but beware. If you follow them rigidly you may end up with 90% like everyone else and 10% really crap.

Deb noticed that Joe's relationship to domestic chores had changed since he started writing crime.....

RULE 22

Tone and style must be consistent

As readers and writers, we often gravitate towards a certain genre, style or tone and the struggles and puzzles of life represented there. Particular features might appeal to us for emotional, cognitive, cultural or ideological reasons. Our needs are not fixed and genre isn't fixed either. In much of what we read and see, we expect to find differences alongside recognisable aspects. Consistency is a kind of uber-rule here; sticking to the rules once you've made them so that everyone knows where they are. Lucy Prebble shares her experience.

> 'I would say I have felt a continued and possibly good pressure in theatre to conform to finding a consistent tone in a play. I have always had notes back on everything I've written, saying that it feels like it's not sure which play it is, and that there is a mix of naturalism and physical and experimental strangeness that does not hang well together. I have swung between agreeing with the note and wondering if that really matters. But it is something I note as being a very powerful need for readers and possibly audiences, I don't know, for formal consistency within one work, over almost anything else. Which I find interesting.'

Most new writers play with tone and style in order to understand the palette. Mastery lies in knowing how to use these discoveries. We've all read or seen work in which a new writer's inconsistent tone or style reflected a lack of craft or precision. New writers may also innovate because they don't know the rules. If they are particularly talented, it may be precisely through their unknowing that they stumble upon something new.

As you become more experienced as a writer, you find that your knowledge of style and genre deepens and your understanding of tonal shifts becomes more subtle. Competence also has its challenges as Neil Hunter, screenwriter and director of *Sparkle* (2007), explains:

> 'I think half the job of writing a screen play is working out the rules of the particular characters and world you are trying to create. And once you have your rules you have your borders and your world becomes more specific and more real. However as someone who accidentally wrote a rom-com I can attest to the almost irresistible force of familiar grooves. You have to fight quite hard not to tumble into them. Film is endlessly plastic and absorbs the unconventional with amazing ease. What feels bold on the page can play surprisingly smoothly on screen. Which means you may have to turn the volume up higher than you think (if you want people to notice which maybe you shouldn't…).'

If you're a rule breaker, you may face the unjust criticism of inconsistency for your daring deviations. Also, experiments do go wrong. You've mixed up conventions or devices in a way that jars but fails to throw light. Your feeling towards the material seems to lurch so drastically that we don't trust the integrity of your voice.

Integrity, openness, curiosity and mastery are perhaps the cornerstones of continuous innovation. Consciously subverting the rule of formal consistency has produced some of the most outstandingly original writing across all media, not least from the imagination of playwright and screenwriter Anthony Neilson. There are few writers in any medium whose work demonstrates such mastery of storytelling and genre alongside such a rare spirit of experiment and a desire to serve their audience with an unforgettable experience.

'Of all the supposed 'rules' of good writing, consistency of tone and style is the one I most consistently break. I have done this throughout my work in a variety of ways. For example, in *The Censor,* I jettisoned the cerebral debate about art halfway through in favour of the 'love' story. In *Relocated,* I used the horror genre to explore a certain mental space, a traumatized life and some people found that offensive. Partly this unpredictability is about delivering shocks – formal, tonal or 'moral', which scramble an audience's cerebral defences and leave them more susceptible to images and feelings.'

I commissioned and produced *The Censor* (1997) and I will never forget the first night. The atmosphere in the audience was electric. *Oh, you're really doing that? Is that possible? Wow!* What Anthony says of his work is true to my own experience of watching it. His shocks have a primal impact. They take you back to a more childlike, immediate state where you experience rather than judge. This is in conscious opposition to the emotionally disconnected traditions that tend to hold sway in British theatre – whether conservative or experimental – reflecting as they do, middle-class culture.

Formal consistency invites familiarity, even a sense of ownership. Breaking that faith can be liberating and offer a different sense of belonging. I expect Anthony's work to break the rules and influence the future of the form. His consistent overturning of conventions feels coherent because of his distinctive voice and vision.

Trojan Horse

Television can feel authoritarian in the way it fixes genre boundaries – for example with continuing drama, the view of the audience seems rather paternalistic. Pre-watershed soaps tread an unambiguous moral line. Justin Young wrote a wonderful cross-genre walkabout play for us when I was running Soho Theatre – *Moonwalking in Chinatown* (2007). Now Series Producer and

Head Writer on BBC's *Holby City*, he explains how he still plays with genre within a generic format.

> 'You can think of it as a Trojan horse; I've written political thrillers and romantic comedies within the format of *Holby City* and because I've worked them into the pre-existing format, I've had the joy of seeing them broadcast on BBC1 with great actors delivering my lines rather than languishing in a desk drawer. Almost always, ironically perhaps, the most successful episodes we broadcast are the most idiosyncratic, the most 'authored'. Authenticity of emotion and passion for characters pings off the page, and if it's not on the page, it won't be on the screen.'

If you seriously want to play with genre it helps to understand what has gone before; to master the kind of subject matter, setting or structure, the characters' desires or dilemmas, the formal conventions – tone, style, theme, tropes. This enables you to play on your audience's expectations.

Translations

Some writers would argue that it's constricting to even talk about genre, we don't need to understand it at all. To test the value of understanding genre, consider a context in which your genre guard is down. For example, when exposed to work in a language and culture not your own.

When I was in South Korea, I was taken to see an unknown play which I immediately recognised as Enda Walsh's *Walworth Farce*. It worked brilliantly; the Irish characters were Filipinos, migrant workers in Seoul. I knew immediately what I was watching from the style and tone of the work. In Southern India, I had almost the opposite genre experience, when I was invited to sit in on the rehearsal of a one-woman Sanskrit piece. I couldn't translate her hand gestures, could only vaguely guess at the story. I needed an understanding of the genre and style to unlock the meaning of the work. Still, I was moved to tears by the passion and exquisite precision of her performance. Lack of knowledge of the genre left me with many questions as to why it worked in the way it did, but that didn't stop the work affecting me on a universal emotional level.

Most writers encounter their new worlds primarily through emotion, whether mastering a new form or searching for innovation. You can choose to arouse certain emotions through stylistic or tonal consistency. You might also break or bypass emotional expectations in order to tap into the primal feelings of the reader-audience. The rule-breaking mastery seems to be about how far you can go in disrupting formal consistency whilst retaining a consistently subversive voice.

RULE BREAKER 22

Subvert formal consistency to free your audience-reader

RULE 23

Keep your language fresh, original and vivid

This rule is true for all writing but especially prose fiction, which relies solely on words. A novel must sustain inventive language that appears to flow from a unique and vivid vision of the world. However, at the heart of any writer's creative process and endeavour, there is a tension between a confident ease of expression and an arresting use of language; between persuading us to look at something we already know and enabling us to perceive it in an entirely new way. As Viktor Shklovsky said, 'art exists that one may recover the sensation of life; it exists to make one feel things, to make the stone stony.'[16] As writers we seek to resensitise humanity through language, but we'll each have a different take on that challenge. How to balance novelty with accessibility? Inventiveness with economy? Is there a point at which story immersion and linguistic innovation are incompatible? What's the relationship between familiar and unfamiliar? Is automatic writing or painstaking construction the key to original language?

Clichés

One of George Orwell's famous rules for writers was 'Never use a metaphor, simile, or other figure of speech which you are used to seeing in print.' If words are too familiar, they are bleached of their emotional riches. Clichés are no longer really experienced by the reader at all.

Hattie Naylor, multi-award-winning writer for radio and stage, takes issue with this prohibition and makes the case for reconnecting her audience with cliché.

> 'Fresh, original and vivid text can be unrelenting if it is not set against banality and cliché, the juxtaposition of the ordinary against the vivid can suddenly illuminate text – in *Play* by Samuel Beckett, the phrase 'I smelt her on him' is set against his distilled text – suddenly illuminating its beauty. In my play *Ivan and the Dogs* this happens for the same reason with bacon crisps. Again it is a distilled play with heightened, lyrical, almost poetic language throughout.'

The point Hattie makes of course, stems from the same desire as Orwell (and Shklovsky) to defamiliarise our relationship to what we know, so that we see and feel anew. In Hattie's example, fresh life is breathed into cliché through its startling proximity to poetry.

Your unique relationship to language

All writers love words and the way we each use language is naturally distinctive to each of us. It is a physical process connected to our breath – in terms of force, rhythm, flow. It is a visual process – we write in pictures that we conjure and experience as we express them. It is a sensory and an emotional process – the words we use have precise associations, feelings and meanings that connect to memory, world view and desire for the future.

Booker shortlisted novelist M.J. Hyland's language feels effortlessly fresh and tactile, yet she works hard to create its heartbreaking impact. It is her precise handling of language and her attention to emotional detail in novels such as *This is How* and *Carry Me Down* that give her work a ferocious poetic force. She explains a breakthrough on her writing journey.

'When I was a young writer, I suffered from two unhelpful and paralysing obsessions. The first, that a very good writer must produce killer opening sentences, and the second, that a great writer must regularly conjure staggering similes and metaphors. These two mistaken notions gave rise to hundreds of months of wasted and misdirected effort. In my twenties, I made a dumb mess; wasted tons of time glued to the hope that I must prove my talent by writing great openings and that I must stick super similes and metaphors in every paragraph. I now know that it's possible to write great fiction without doing very much of either, and more, that unless a writer has a natural gift for simile and metaphor, he should quit going after them. The writer with no knack for these things must work instead for authentic and truthful storytelling. As for killer openings, they are rare for good reason. And as for bad similes and metaphors, there's likewise a good reason that they rage like locusts in the pages of all mediocre fiction, and can even be seen crawling the walls of the finest literary rooms. You see what I mean.'

You can only express your voice truthfully by freeing it from perfectionist expectation, your own or others. Confidence lies at the heart of creativity and self-belief gives license. I find Maria's experience hugely reassuring. Her work is no less poetic for its emphasis on storytelling and her own journey confirms how pointless and destructive it can be to turn the achievements of one kind of writer into rules for another.

Standards of economy and clarity

Many writers have put forward rules aimed at inspiring clear, economic, inventive use of language. Some of Orwell's and V.S. Naipaul's rules for new writers are included in the list below. These common prescriptions won't support your first draft, though they might help your rewrites if used judiciously. One way to test them out for yourself is to take an old piece of prose, rewrite according to this checklist and assess the difference. You'll no doubt feel some improvement and you'll gain awareness of style habits, but remember to count your losses too. Rules exist to be broken. The rules are in bold, my comments are not.

- **Write in short sentences**. Disciplined but limiting. It gains pace. It's forceful. But variety is the key to engagement.
- **Better to have no more than three sentences in any speech**. This is taught in TV and no doubt elsewhere. Thankfully often broken, so take the point about economy, then ignore.
- **Never use a long word when a short one will do** (Orwell). **Even difficult ideas can be broken down into small words** (V.S. Naipaul). I'm glad Shakespeare didn't follow this rule wholesale. Aim for simplicity but also enjoy the richness of your language.
- **Never use the passive where you can use the active** (Orwell). Sure, active voice is stronger and more energized, and on balance you will no doubt use it more, but sometimes, slowing the narrative down, weakening or creating emotional detachment with passive voice can be exactly what you need.
- **Avoid lists of adjectives**. Helpful advice in creating taut prose and concrete description, but see the quotation from *Obsession* on page 166 for a modern rule-breaker that works, though of course it is in free verse rather than prose…
- **The beginner should avoid using adjectives, except those of colour, size and number** (V.S. Naipaul). This exercise may cure excesses and addictions. It may also stifle your joy and freedom in writing.
- **Strong verbs are the key to robust writing.** It is through action that the story is told, but this rule can be taken to ludicrous extremes, where adjectival and adverbial absence puts all the pressure for vividness upon the verb. What's wrong with 'To be, or not to be'?

- **Only modify with an adverb if you can't find the perfect verb**. Getting rid of adverbs gives your storytelling impact and precision, but uniformity is also dull.
- **Don't use qualifiers with 'said'.** 'She said angrily' for example. This rule says that the character's anger should be implicit in the dialogue or the action taking place around it. The equivalent of this rule in drama is to erase those annoying directions before the line telling the actor how to say it *(angrily)*. An exception in drama might be a major shift of emotional gear that needs emphasis for an actor to understand. Sometimes in prose a need for clarity will justify this too. This rule is about fashion as much as economy.
- **Don't replace 'said' with another verb**. I'm amused by the rules around the supposedly invisible 'said'. When I was at school, the rule was *never* to use 'said' in a story because it was boring. Rules eh? 'Only use said' has become the norm, so surely some deviation is welcome? In the same way that too much ping-pong dialogue makes you yawn at conflict, too much stripping back of prose denudes the language.

Linguistic riches

Of all writers, Shakespeare has had the most remarkable influence on English language and literature. It was the lack of rules around language, the absence of standardization that enabled such linguistic verve. Around 10% of words in his plays were new to his audience,[17] sometimes culled from foreign languages or the classics. He used nouns as verbs or verbs as adjectives. He also made words up. No one told Shakespeare to cut the adjectives and find the right verb instead; at least if they did he took no notice.

Another astonishing thing about Shakespeare is that he didn't rewrite his plays, at least not in the solitary way that a modern playwright might. Along with borrowing plotlines and passages from other writers, this explains how he could be so prolific. Those exquisite, sensitive images simply flowed, alongside the kind of shockingly bad writing you expect from a first draft. His actors honed the material through performance.

Shakespeare combined an ability to express a complex, contradictory thought in a few words with a genius for metaphor – his images multiply in meaning as they are spoken. This speech from *King Lear* is a great example of a passionate writer visualizing truthful feeling and summoning up the words to say it, letting the anger rip through his character and arousing that of the audience. Lear has seen his own tyranny in the actions of his daughters and watched power destroy compassion. He finally sees the full injustice of the world, but now being powerless, he can only rail against it.

> Thou rascal beadle, hold thy bloody hand!
> Why dost thou lash that whore? Strip thine own back;
> Thou hotly lust'st to use her in that kind
> For which thou hast whipp'st her. The userer hangs the cozener.
> Through tatter'd clothes small vices do appear;
> Robes and furr'd gowns hide all. Plate sin with gold,
> And the strong lance of justice hurtless breaks;
> Arm it in rags, a pygmy's straw does pierce it.
> None does offend, none. – I say none;

Shakespeare comes at the same idea repeatedly here through distinct but connected images. One way to find a fresh language for a stale passage or scene is to do what Shakespeare did within his extraordinary first drafts and write from a new perspective, mood, time of day, place, genre or style. Rewrite in yellow, hostility, touch, sunset, desert, operatic or whatever you like. It's an old rehearsal trick if a path becomes too well-trodden and it works to reinvigorate writing too, reintroducing playfulness, enabling you to see it freshly.

In theatre, words live in the air between performer and audience, heightened by the vocal power needed to convey them. It's a medium made for poetry of all kinds, a dream where the known is made strange. Like a great literary metaphor, a stage setting or object can transform before our eyes, accumulating multiple meanings. For example in Philip Ridley's *Piranha Heights* we hear about a baby belonging to two teenagers. When they wheel in 'Bubba' in his pram it is a doll. The symbolic representation of a baby by a doll is a common theatrical convention, but in the reality of this story it is in fact a doll being treated by the teenagers as if it were a baby. The final twist comes when Bubba is beheaded by his 'dad', Medic, and we share the horror of 'mum', Lilly, who believes it is their real baby, which in a sense it is.

In all modes of creative writing you face the challenge of conveying in words on the page what the audience will see in pictures. This is as much about the absence of words as the choice of words and the linguistic skill needed is distinct to each medium. In prose fiction, what you don't say is for the reader alone to fill in as they imagine and it's a question of just the right amount of detail. In dramatic writing these words serve quite a different function, inspiring the creative interpretation of other artists rather than the audience. Particularly in screenwriting the art is to enable the evocation of visual images that may expand or contradict the dialogue and not simply emphasise or repeat it. In this way screenwriting is the most concentrated and poetic form.

Your unique relationship to language is the key to original writing but this comes from a place beyond words. It comes through the pleasure and discipline of practice, through honing your dispassionate take on the world and liberating your passionate inner voice. You may need to free your expression from habitual linguistic patterns but automatic writing can be as helpful in this as conscious effort (**Rule 2**). Most writers use a combination of both. Wherever your love of language leads you, let words start with truthful feeling, clearly experienced through all the senses. This is the key to vivid writing.

RULE BREAKER 23

Original language starts with the force of feeling

RULE 24

The writer is the invisible hand

The artist like the God of his creation, remains within or behind or beyond his handiwork, invisible, refined out of existence, indifferent, paring his fingernails.

James Joyce, *A Portrait of the Artist as a Young Man*[18]

Aristotle complains that in the epic 'Some writers are forever striding into their own compositions, allowing little scope for creation.'[19] The distanced, confident omniscient narrator of the British 19th-century novel assumes not just a right but a duty to take the high moral ground. In the 20th century however, part of the pact of the omniscient narrator intimately entering the minds of their characters is that we only see through the characters' eyes (as well as judging their speech and actions). The writer's judgement of their characters is always implicit but if they interrupt their own work to comment then we may feel cheated out of the imaginative illusion. Our ownership has been stolen, the writer has taken unfair advantage of their omniscience in demanding that we listen to their other reality. Haven't they heard that God and the author are dead?[20] Is it true that paradoxically, the more visible the author is in their narrative, the less they are believed?

Though novelists' opinions may rarely grace the pages of their fiction, they will be expected to offer them on every other platform. Intentions and viewpoints are a marketing opportunity. So are there rule-breakers for this invisibility within the work, contrasting so poignantly with the demand for comment beyond it?

Celebrated novelist and cultural critic Edmund White successfully and subtly subverts the trend of the invisible author.

> 'Most 20th-century writing in English has done away with epigrams and apothegms, all those nuggets of 'wisdom' that ornamented 18th- and 19th-century novels. I suppose the idea was that it wasn't 'cool' to have opinions about life and love stated in so many words as the author's own views. Maybe it was James Joyce's ideal of the author standing outside his text, refined out of existence, paring his nails, that inspired this view of artistic inscrutability, or maybe it was Henry James' dramatic method in which every utterance is supposed to be made from a single character's point of view in order to express that character's take on the action and nothing else. I was certainly influenced when I was young by James, but in my thirties I read Elizabeth Bowen's masterpieces, *The House in Paris* and *The Death of the Heart*, and I was deeply impressed by her direct statement of her subtle, penetrating views on human nature. After that, for better or for worse, I no longer feared speaking my own mind in a piece of fiction. The trick, as Bowen had demonstrated, was how to get into and out of such statements gracefully and deftly, without slowing the pace of the narration. Without bragging I think I succeeded; at least no critic has ever taken me to task for 'philosophising', nor has anyone ever mentioned that I do such a thing.'

Disguising your ideology as fiction does have certain political advantages. The character rather than the author is responsible – a useful defence when free speech is under attack. In Iran, I was fascinated to see how extant texts were used to promote contemporary oppositional views and deny personal authorship. 'It wasn't me it was Shakespeare!' Metaphor allows you to present plausible alternative interpretations to the censor. Or at least that's the theory. I was queuing for a show at City Theatre in Tehran when I witnessed the actors of a highly inventive adaptation of *King Lear* emerging miserably from a studio. The ensemble had to perform the play three times for the censors and cuts were being made. I wondered whether the unforgettable scene where Cordelia whimpers as she is flogged in prison in pitch darkness might be deemed unacceptable on stage, though the Iranian government finds it acceptable to enact such scenes in reality.

Post-structuralist critics since Barthes have ridiculed any identification of the person of the author with the work. Both are just 'unstable texts'. Meaning is left to 'the birth of the reader.' In one sense this is a continuation of the trend whereby the author's labour is no longer visible. On the other hand, in experimental writing, the structure itself may become the subject matter and there are slippages across many realities, including the boundary between author and character. This actively and deliberately challenges the non-critical suspension of disbelief of the reader and the absence of the author.

RULE BREAKER 24

Show your hand without showing off

RULE 25

Less is More

This rule of economy is about using the fewest words for the most precise, impactful meaning. However, its application intersects with taste in a particular way too.

Writing economically is covered in other sections, for example **Rules 11, 23** and **26**. Here are some additional **Less is More** tips.

- Less description. In novels be ruled by what it adds to the story or reveals of character. Always be specific. Cut adjectives and adverbs. In playwriting and screenwriting don't overload with visual descriptions or explicit directions for camera or actors. Instead, direct your reader to see it that way. Remember that a team of people, also artists, will be working from feelings and instincts after reading your script.

- Fewer characters. New writers are often tempted to overpopulate their work because it's easier to bring in new dynamics than deepen existing ones. Watch out for too many antagonists, supporters or mentors repeating one another's function in the story.

- Less coming and going. Often exits and entrances are unnecessary and the scene can just start in the middle. Here the convention of film has been hugely influential on the novel and stage play with everything written in visual action scenes.

- Less of the same thing. Two of the same are often not as strong as one and three becomes a cliché. The more potent or remarkable the element, the more sparing you must be to retain its power. This applies to unusual adjectives, magical devices, life-threatening illnesses, metaphors and more. Cut or alter repetition of information, meaning, emotional conflict: sound of names, favourite words, character needs, storylines, actions; length of scene, chapter or beat. Of course keep the deliberate, meaningful repetition that you've used poetically for rhythm or emphasis.

- Fewer words. Try cutting at least half of any scene that feels stodgy. See the scene as you cut as well as hear what's being said, whatever medium you're in. You need to feel what's right so as not to lose the heart of it, the atmosphere, rhythm or texture.

More is More

Ask yourself what you lose by culling. Often you gain, but not always. The effect of your economy drive may be to close the gap between significant story beats and increase the pace. But sometimes, to increase engagement you need to *open* the story gap. Scenes can be underwritten as well as overwritten. We might need to know more detail about characters, a place or an action.

By *adding* material we can also increase the sense of pace, unlikely though it sounds. This is because being immersed in the work completely alters an audience-reader's sense of time. When we are living with the picture, moment to moment through present action, fictional time expands and real time disappears more quickly. Where did the time go? We were lost in the story or performance.

Excess can be self-indulgent and tip a serious work into comedy. On the other hand there are glorious maximalists who revel in this and playfully use it to embrace an altered state that delights in abundance and over-use of the same element. The first half of Anthony Neilson's *The Wonderful World of Dissocia* (**Rule 27**) is a kind of modern-day *Alice's Adventures in Wonderland*, where more is more is used to express a delusional manic state.

RULE BREAKER 25

More is More

RULE 26

Show don't tell

Don't tell me the moon is shining; show me the glint of light on broken glass.

Anton Chekhov

This famous quote from Chekhov implies a deeper, more democratic engagement. Showing may be just as manipulative as telling but somehow it *seems* less didactic, it invites participation. Your audience-reader feels trusted to make up their own mind based on what they experience, and they have a greater sense of ownership over the shown world. At least that's the theory. Award-winning novelist and critic Neel Mukherjee disputes this.

'Rubbish, absolute rubbish. This is one of those idiocies-masquerading-as-wisdom that has come out of creative writing school factories and seems to have developed frighteningly tenacious staying power. Don't believe it. While the (limited) application of the tenet to a situation where you show someone wolfing down eight bananas, a bag of chips and half a cow in ten minutes flat rather than write, 'He was ravenous', works well enough, any narrative requires you to give information by some straightforward telling. How do you release historical information in a novel? Or what about when a first-person narrator speaks? That is nothing but telling.

In the first and second narratives, both first-person accounts, in V.S. Naipaul's *In a Free State*, the entire story is 'told' by one person, not 'shown'. Isn't dialogue a way of telling too? Often it can become expository, plodding, an ill-disguised attempt to give information which could have been more honestly given by straightforward omniscient narration. Once again, *In A Free State* serves as a superb model: the final, eponymous novella sketches out a deep understanding of both the political state of the country in which the characters are driving through *and* their fractious, problematic positions in it through the business of two people talking; not for half a line does it descend into history lesson or filling in context and background information. It does this by two people 'telling' each other things. Or think of the novels of Javier Marías, where you get page after page of the intricacies of someone's thought process. Ditto Henry James.

The 'show, not tell' orthodoxy seems to have arisen out of a misplaced desire to see the novel approach the condition of film or drama, different forms altogether, with different languages. It is a symptom of impatience, the need for instant gratification, a bending of the knees at the altar of that wicked false god, Accessibility. Which is why the Anglo-Saxon novel has remained stuck stuck stuck with the realist model of plot-character-dialogue. Elsewhere, the frontiers are being pushed to create exciting, new forms out of the novel. To read just one such contemporary novelist, Jenny Erpenbeck from Germany, is to be reminded of such possibilities.'

Neel points up the difference here between the conventions of prose fiction and drama regarding **Show don't tell**. One fundamental distinction is that a fiction writer will tend to use more words to show than tell and a dramatist more words to tell than show. On this basis alone, a novel could not credibly only show – the expansion of time needed for the depth of detail would be quite off-putting.

However, similar issues do arise across the forms. Showing something in drama for example, can still be about telling – such as an establishing shot in film or the times when less accomplished dramatists make their characters self-narrate. I also find myself wondering about Neel's assertion that the idea of accessibility is related to 'show.' It may be true in terms of immediacy in prose fiction, but in drama there is usually more room for interpretation when you 'show.' 'Tell' can be pretty unambiguous in terms of literal or expositional material.

When telling is showing

It depends what we mean by telling or showing. As Neel points out you can't get more telling than first-person narrative. So let's take the following example from *Obsession* (1996) by Rob Young – a monologue that I directed many moons ago. We spend an hour with a masochistic man who is obsessively in love with an apparently sadistic woman. Our interest lies in what the man *shows* us about himself through *telling* us about her. As Rob observes:

> 'When writing a monologue, it's easy to fall into the trap of thinking that you're writing for one voice, when the truth is, you are always writing for two. Even if it's just someone standing there, wrestling with their own inner demons, that's still a dialogue.'

In these early lines we are being shown the character's inner conflict.

Her eyes register no emotion

Nothing unresolved grey weak ammonia eyes
Accusing punishing dirty little penknife eyes
Too far apart
I can hear them
Buzzing
Her eyelids clicking against them like moths

Her voice is like bathing in lukewarm water
Clipped acidic articulate intelligent barbed forced
Her silences are loaded
Her reassurances calculated
And words given as small unsatisfying gifts

She has wrinkles
They emphasize her youth

Her hands are cold spaghetti
White vein tapestry
Kitchen skin

Her fingernails clatter
Like chopsticks
They can open pistachios
They could open a tin

I love her
I love her

The images conjured up are far funnier/sadder than being shown the real woman. Undoubtedly, if we saw her, she would seem perfectly normal, not this monster that lives in the mind of the man. Being told about her allows room for interpretation, mainly because there is a disjuncture between what we are being told and what we are implicitly shown – the man's disturbed mental state.

Balancing show and tell

- Sometimes, telling is about a shortcut you took when writing your first draft quickly, and now you need to go back and experience the moment more fully, go right into it, show it vividly. This might be about allowing your characters to think and say stuff instead of you narrating it or about adding emotional beats or specific details to the picture. Sometimes, breaking up narrative chunks reveals to you how little you need them. Sometimes you do just need to tell it, but with a sense of what you're showing us, as in the above example of *Obsession*.
- In prose fiction, a mixture of showing and telling is always needed; the balance between visual scene and narrative

summary; between creating sensory immersion and moving the story on.

- Though we've asserted that telling can also be action, characters are often defined better through an action expressing how they feel. For example, a character punches a wall with her fist instead of saying 'I'm angry.' On the other hand, characters are also defined through intention, through striving. Their lack of ability to clearly act may be shown or told to create conflict.
- Let other stuff do the talking. Show us the environment your characters inhabit, the gestures your characters make, their physical actions. Let another character offer insight into your main character. In prose fiction, find places to replace speaker attribution with action, just be selective.
- Ensure that the scene is actually about the people in it. Try not to let one character tell another character what they already know for the sake of telling the audience-reader. Maintain the integrity of the story, beat to beat.
- Sometimes, even on stage, you *do* just need to simply tell it straight. Literal exposition can be the best choice. For example, in Kay Adshead's *The Bogus Woman* (2001), the young woman introduces us to a shocking image:

Campsfield Detention Centre
A tangled tower
Of twenty foot high razor wire

- Sometimes, if you need to tell rather than show, it can work to use characters who are in a good position to ask questions. Just beware of falling into the cliché of peopling your work with kids, cops and shrinks to serve your telling purpose!
- Avoid using dialogue to tell us what we could work out for ourselves. A lesson from acting that also holds for writing is that the deepest meaning lies in what the character *conceals* through the action they are playing.

- In your novel, are you using italicised inner monologue to show what would be better told? It's not a great place to hide telling exposition – too emotionally immediate. In drama you can hide information more easily in emotionally charged moments since the focus will be on the emotion shown, rather than the facts told. Take this example from the play *Baghdad Wedding*, where Marwan is trying to persuade Luma to leave Iraq with him rather than marry Salim. Their heated exchange conveys vital information about life for women in Iraq that was not common knowledge in the UK at that time. Concealed within the action of the love story, it becomes part of Marwan's ammunition.

LUNA: …Someone needs to scream at the top of their lungs about what is happening.

MARWAN: What good will that do? No really, tell me. You think the problem is a shortage of words? Half the Amazon rainforest has gone into writing about Iraq. *(Pause)* A maniac could walk in here one day and gun you down…all because you are not wearing the veil. Married or not.[21]

- Voiceover narratives in film and radio or long narrative summaries in novels *can* work beautifully, but not if they simply appear to plug the info gap or because you're not trusting the audience to work it out. Make sure you know why the narrative is there. When you summarise situations or characters you run the risk of over-simplifying them.

Show the telling turning points

The most satisfying way to use exposition is as part of your story design. *Orphans* and *Never Let Me Go Two* are just two works referenced in this book that structure turning points around telling revelations. Both use exposition as revelation throughout the story too. At the big changes on a character's journey they are forced into a new action, can no longer accept the status quo. Sometimes the shift is in the reader-audience's insight rather than the character's. We need to fully experience these moments, so it's usually best to show us the action. Then, when the desire to know has been brought to optimum point, tell us the surprising secret.

RULE BREAKER 26

It's the way you tell 'em

RULES 27-31

Principles of Freedom: Written and Unwritten Laws of Taste and Taboos

This section is about the power of the dominant culture and its gatekeepers. I will draw on my own experience as an artistic director most fully here, but also that of writers working in different media.

RULE 27

Obey the arbiters of taste

I want to stay as close to the edge as I can without going over. Out on the edge you see all kinds of things you can't see from the center.

Kurt Vonnegut, *Player Piano*

This rule about taste is an unwritten one and therefore slippery, but it is probably the most influential rule in this book. In nearly all contexts, arbiters of taste sit between your work and your reader-audience. Who are these 'gatekeepers'? The people who buy, produce and distribute your work; producers, directors, publishers, agents, editors, literary managers, executives and boards. Then there are the critics, the people who decide whether your writing is successful in the world. Finally there is the critical mass – your reader-audience.

Some archetypal gatekeepers

Gatekeepers who…

…don't know their own taste.

only know what sold well in the past.

are pragmatic and risk-averse.

play the system and occasionally succeed for the writer.

are writer-centred.

are visionary and overtly challenge the system.

Real gatekeepers tend to cross these categories. For example, in theatre there are some literary gatekeepers who are sensitive to writers but don't have the experience to read a play as living theatre. In TV there are those executives who want a fresh and original show mixing the successful aspects of two shows they did last year.

Gatekeepers as arbiters of taste

The criteria for success are your own. However, pronouncements on your work and its sales will influence future opportunities, so you need either money or courage to ignore the gatekeepers. Great writers are generally brave in this respect and keep going regardless of the many hurdles.

Let's assume that you are talented and original. You have a great idea or first draft. It's been a long haul to get from a blank sheet of paper to the gatekeepers, but you've done it! Let's imagine that your work does something unsettling. Perhaps it's provocative, it breaks a basic convention or maybe your process is high risk (**Rule 6**). How do you convince the gatekeepers of the potential success of your brilliant rule-breaking work? What if you can't?

Writer and performer Penny Pepper explains the issue with her current novel:

> 'Disability, as the world misunderstands it, is still a dirty word. The fully fleshed, rounded experiences of disabled people such as myself are not exposed to a wider public, even though we are part of that public and the human condition.
>
> From an early age I wrote about the untold. When I was all growed up I dared to bring sex into the mix. Naughty Penny. This came out in a torrent of personal insurrection against the view that disabled people were asexual. My collection of erotica *Desires* (originally called *Cripples Fucking*) met with shock and disbelief from mainstream publishers, and was only published with the help of the Arts Council.
>
> At present, my current novel *Fancy Nancy*, is doing the slow rounds; a crazy tale of Victorian freak shows, paralleled with the daily traumas of life in 21st-century Britain. Like most of my work, it is rude, it is real. It is my life and that of others in my ghetto. Publishers squirm at my non-PC language, the bawdy sex. One called the

disability references crass. This is not so much a glass
ceiling, but a challenging of history.'

I can't think of a more blatant example of a gatekeeper excluding
a writer's work from cultural distribution on the basis of taste.

What is taste?

When we talk about taste as if it is simply a personal response,
we are only partially correct. For the gatekeepers, taste is a kind
of unspoken, often unconscious trending, to which writers are
held to ransom. If the Arts Council decides it is giving money
to digital this year, then almost every piece of theatre you see
will have a digital element. If a TV company decides it wants
supernatural, that's what you'll be pitching.

Anthony Neilson sees it like this:

> 'Taste is a pernicious system of control, an attempt to
> inhibit our ability to reflect or oppose the truth. The most
> important rules to break are the ones we set ourselves;
> the ones that we know will invite ridicule from our
> peers, really risk us, hurt us as we break them.'

This goes to the heart of what it means to create, to sacrifice
ego for what the work demands. Other people's taste can get in
the way of a vision, the obsessive pursuit of truthfully creating
a unique world. Being an artist is not about popularity and it
is painful to test your own belief or completely overturn it; to
remain singular, open and self-critical. Anthony goes further:

> 'I feel bravest when I know that people will misunderstand
> what I'm doing, but I'm often doing it to create an
> emotional effect. For example, in the first half of *The
> Wonderful World of Dissocia*, I remember thinking that it
> went on too long and I was going to cut it, but then I
> realized that you needed to get irritated by it. If it had
> been a perfect length you wouldn't have wanted to get rid
> of it. By the end of the second half, the audience, whose

patience had been tried by the first half, already wanted to go back there. Doing the wrong thing was kind of the right thing. People talk about audience participation, but the fourth wall that needs breaking is the one in the audience's minds.'

We all have feelings about the world we live in that inform our response to art. That is why work which scrambles an audience-reader's sense of itself can be so powerful, and why, as Anthony Neilson explains, it is also hugely challenging and important to put oneself on the line for that. I believe this is why critics have rarely understood Anthony's work even though many would recognise that he is one of the most important playwrights in the UK today.

Theatre critics have a paradoxical job. In the UK they judge work, when, at its best, theatre bypasses rational critical paradigms – the fourth wall that Anthony describes breaking. There are critics who have truly dedicated their lives to theatre – they are erudite and have an encyclopedic knowledge. However, some are lost with innovation because they study a medium that you can only deeply appreciate through immersion and primal creative engagement. Critics don't behave like a paying audience and if they thought like one, would be out of a job. There is a tendency to applaud literal, cerebral work or spectacle – work which requires less emotional investment. The result is too frequently a hyping of mediocrity.

I'm not bashing theatre critics here. It was a senior reviewer who pointed out to me that most of his colleagues simply didn't understand new writing. Some critics do write creatively themselves or are involved in the theatre-making process and this helps. Perhaps it would serve theatre to bring some critics together for a playwriting workshop…

One of the tests of a great play is how long it stays with you – something critics can't judge in a review. Perhaps this is why they applaud polished product, whereas I think the most interesting writers and artists of all kinds, rebel against the notion of that. If it's polished, scratch it. Live Artist Stacy Makishi echoes Anthony's sentiments from a different angle.

> 'It's not always obvious to know when it's time to break a rule. For me, a flag goes off when my writing becomes 'too right' and I'm overly protective about sticking to a rule. When this happens, I break the rule by doing the exact opposite. For instance, if the rule is to make a series of smooth transitions from one idea to the next, I'll break the rule by creating a series of ruptures where there are no transitions at all. I'll write a series of paragraphs or singular words where one subject collides directly with another. Sometimes new life and meaning can emerge between the cracks. Writing is strongest where something was once broken.'

We break through the old self to keep creating, just making sure that we don't break ourselves apart in the process (**Rule 37**). I agree with Stacy's idea that something must be broken if it becomes too aligned with the status quo of taste. I identify with this as a director – trashing perfect moments is part of my process too. Polishing performance for the sake of it closes down possibilities. Keeping work alive, growing and listening is the most important thing for me, maintaining that raw energy. Of course if slick is the right artistic choice for the material, then let's do it, but not as a default position. That would be like stopping at the first hurdle.

Bringing the edge to the centre

Gatekeepers can work like artists if they choose to, however harsh the constraints. I know I consciously did. As Artistic Director at Soho Theatre I remember having a feeling of liberation when with Paul Sirett I co-translated and programmed Dorota Masłowka's wild and unique *A Couple of Poor Polish-Speaking Romanians* with the brilliant Andrea Riseborough and Andrew Tiernan in the lead roles. I'd had a first year of sell-out, critically acclaimed shows. I remember someone saying to me 'if you're selling out you're not taking enough risks' and

I couldn't get that out of my head. I consciously pulled the rug from under myself because the programme seemed too perfect, too sure of itself. More risk was needed.

That is a mental process that a marketeer or board might find hard to understand, but from a cultural point of view it makes sense. This was the first Polish Gen X play to be put on in London, attracting a young Polish audience. Our version of the play has since been performed in America, Australia and Ireland. Brian Logan, himself a playwright, performer and critic pointed out my risk-taking as a gatekeeper in a *New Statesman* interview, though one might legitimately ask where the risk he speaks of lies. Perhaps simply with the taste of other gatekeepers.

> 'Goldman has transformed the venue, making it a home to radical international drama, where exiled Iraqi authors hobnob with the dissenting Belarus Free Theatre (banned in its home country), where a Gen X Polish wunderkind gets her British premiere and where a troupe of Anglo-German performance artists (Gob Squad), renowned across Europe, is given a rare UK outing. That does not surprise anyone who knows Goldman – who previously ran the politicised Red Room company, and who from 2001 was active in the establishment of Artists Against the War. The surprise was her appointment to Soho in the first place. For all the lip-service paid to 'vision' and 'ambition', mainstream theatres usually place their artistic leadership in the safest possible hands.'[22]

There are many ways for writers to circumvent the arbiters of taste, but most of them involve working unpaid and/or raising investment of money, people, resources. The DIY culture of fringe theatre, self-publishing and guerilla film-making is ever expanding. A lot of this work is aimed at the existing mainstream, but the edge remains the centre of innovation too.

Being a writer is about being yourself and capturing your own changes. Writing reminds you that the world is as you make it, that you can expand your freedom as a human being and share the fruits of your imagination with others. That this freedom may sometimes be curtailed by the establishment using the 'subjective' criteria of taste is neither surprising nor must it hold you back.

RULE BREAKER 27

Influence the taste of the future

RULE 28

Be balanced

Talking about balance in an aesthetic sense is a kind of shorthand for 'what works'. For example, balancing the orchestration of characters; the narrative and dialogue; the inner landscape and external reality. We accept that aesthetic balance is subjective though many of us share notions of beauty and proportion. Well executed work that deliberately tips this balance draws attention to itself and forces us to question our response to art and its place in the world. The balancing act becomes unstable in the slippage between aesthetics and ideology. You may be asked to be more balanced in your writing because the theme or meaning of the work overturns the perceived balance of the status quo. Playwright Oladipo Agboluaje offers his opinion of this.

> 'Balance, in writing, evokes many things, like creating balance between all the aspects of writing a play. In terms of character, for me, balance is more about the characters weighing their choices against other characters and their choices. Giving characters their time on stage is proportional to their relevance to the story; it is not for creating some artificial equality for the sake of expressing a character's humanity. Balance should not inhibit me from expressing my world view as loudly as I can. What determines its volume is the story with which I express my world view. For instance, in *Iya-Ile* quite a few characters compete for stage time. Having the backdrop of a specifically venal and mendacious military government allowed for me to show how the era defined their characters while at the same time express my disgust

for military dictatorships. Balance should not be used as a tool to blunt the writer's opinions. If the taxi driver has an opinion why can't I have one?'

Balance has become the acceptable face of censorship in the UK arts world. It is the compliance units at the BBC; the board member who really doesn't want that kind of work on here; the producer who is scared of unpopularity. Balance means safe and it has the advantage of sounding fair. Critics love this journalistic concept because it gives them a yardstick against which to measure the value of work. Art is not journalism, neither is it fair. Writing fiction is the act of sharing with others a vision, a value, a feeling. It is always subjective.

David Hermanstein raises another aspect of balance. He argues that the diversity of cultural experience in British society is under-represented in TV drama.

> 'Regarding writers of African-Caribbean descent, a simple question could be: is there or has there ever been a long-running series based around a black character or a family? We all know the answer to that. It has always been difficult to have us portrayed with subtlety, complexity and authenticity. It's not that non-black writers can't (or shouldn't) write black characters, it's just that rarely have black writers been given the opportunity to do so. If producers feel there is no need for a proactive search for authentic black voices anymore, they are avoiding the main issue which is as black writers, we've never had any control over how we're portrayed, which is especially hard to take as television is such a wide-reaching, powerful and influential medium. We've never had an influential black figure in television long enough to ensure quality and cement standards. This shouldn't stop us from trying but having worked with and spoken to other black writers, directors and producers about their experiences in television and radio, the process can make one very cynical because there have been instances when at worst, your voice is ignored, at best, your voice is compromised.

This is because producers they have worked with only see the world through the narrow prism of their white middle-class experience, which does not reflect the experiences of the majority of viewers. If they feel such fresh perspectives will alienate viewers, then they ultimately insult the viewers' intelligence. If producers want to reflect viewers, then they'd know that viewers welcome risk, welcome diversity simply because they live it.'

At first sight David appears to be saying the opposite to Dipo, that actually we need a more objective redressing of ideological balance to counter the weight of history, rather than a free subjectivity. However, in talking about balance as either a form of political or cultural exclusion, both writers are exploring the balance of power in our society and the way that the dominant culture silences or excludes opinions that it finds unpalatable or voices that it doesn't understand.

RULE BREAKER 28

Shift the balance of power by saying what isn't said

RULE 29

Do not offend

Taste has its boundaries – what is deemed offensive. This changes with time and context. For example, anti-Semitism was seen as perfectly acceptable in UK society before World War II. When Terence Rattigan co-wrote a witty attack on Nazism in the 1930s, the Lord Chamberlain wouldn't license it because it attacked a foreign power. We need only consider the unfounded accusations of anti-Semitism against playwright Caryl Churchill's *Seven Jewish Children* (2009) to see how establishment thinking has changed.

We live in a society where multiculturalism has become the dominant agenda. These days, a play attacking a foreign power would be less likely to evoke disapproval than one attacking a foreign next-door neighbour. However, the politics of multiculturalism brings contradictory issues to the fore, not least the notion of empowering communities through respecting and upholding their beliefs.

Cultural ignorance or sloppy research demeans writer and reader-audience. However, there is a distinction between cultural authentication and what is deemed acceptable by self-appointed cultural guardians. Communities are not homogeneous. For example, in *Shraddhā* (see page 127), there is a Romany woman whose husband has left her. This is highly unusual within the Romany community and would be frowned upon. If Romanies had been consulted about the 'rightness' of this culturally, some might have objected. Does that mean a Romany woman has never been deserted or that it couldn't happen? Of course not.

Great fiction generally sits at the edge of common experience and writers must be free to invent.

How does this play out when a writer critiques their own community? Consider the furore over Salman Rushdie's *Satanic Verses* (1988), Monica Ali's *Brick Lane* (2003) or Gurpreet Kaur Bhatti's censored *Behzti* (2004). In a case study of Gurpreet's next play *Behud* (2010), writer and commentator Kenan Malik, makes the point that 'in almost every case, what is often called offence to a community is actually a dialogue or debate within that community.'[23]

The desire to be offended has become endemic in the UK. To take offence, a leap of imagination is often required. When my company The Red Room produced *Stitching* by Anthony Neilson, a double-page spread in *The Guardian* complained that a character was masturbating over pictures of the holocaust, though there was no masturbation and no picture. The protests against *Behzti* by a minority of Sikhs were about the reference in the play to a rape in a Gurdwara, a Sikh temple. The rape was never shown on stage and few demonstrators, if any, had seen the show.

Censorship is often covert – not policing by the state but self-policing through the institution. *Behzti* was closed down by Birmingham Rep Theatre on the grounds of 'health and safety'. Gurpreet was forced into hiding after death threats. The case of *Behzti* showed how little regard the institution had for the free expression of the writer. She was simply silenced.

So what is our responsibility to the artist's right to free speech, particularly where this is put to the test? Who, if anyone, should define what is deemed 'offensive'? How does a theatre decide whether or not to consult with a 'community' represented on stage? Indeed should it ever? The closure of *Behzti* sent shockwaves through British theatre and the cause of free artistic expression was pushed back, opening the door to assertive protests against provocative work.

In 2007 Gurpreet approached me with a very rough draft of a satire on these events called *Behud* (trans. Beyond Belief). I felt she deserved her right to reply and that theatre needed to regain ground lost through censorship. Until *Behud* went on, *Behzti* would never be produced again and Gurpreet would not be free to write for theatre about any subject she chose. We developed the project over two years.

Briefly, the story follows the writer-protagonist Tarlochan's attempt to deal with the real event of her censored play *Gund* (trans. Filth) by creating a new play about those events. Gradually she becomes trapped in her own creation and as the levels of reality and fiction multiply, the audience witnesses an artist's psychological breakdown in the face of the unbearable trauma of censorship, and ultimately her survival to continue writing. The play explores self-censorship as well as institutional censorship; the need to express oneself that lies at the root of artistic freedom; the illusion of control; the impact of reality on fiction and fiction on reality.

In the fiction of *Behud* (and in the reality of the production process) theatre managers, boards, local councils, the press and the police are as problematic to the writer as the Sikhs who are against her work. In Gurpreet's play, *as in reality*, the sectional desire to be offended and the institutional desire to be publicly responsible create an interdependent tyranny of consensus against the progressive writer. There is not the space here to tell the whole story of producing *Behud* in 2010, but I have explored it elsewhere and I think it gives an interesting insight into covert censorship and the way institutions think.[24]

Suffice to say the police asked us to pull the production in expectation of violent protests and we refused. Consequently there were 70 police outside Belgrade Theatre Coventry at the first performance and heavy security inside. There were no physical protests at all and the work went ahead.

Gurpreet says:

> 'Words are freedom. They have to be. And writers must have the freedom to explore the extremities of their imagination to provoke and poke around amidst the dirt and filth of the human condition. If not, drama becomes sanitised, homogenous and dull because it is only born of fear. A corrosive fear that is the enemy of true creativity. Do what you want to do, not what anyone thinks you should do. Be brave. Besides, maybe those who oppose genuine debate and dialogue need to be offended.'

Whilst we were busy with *Behud*, a revival of Philip Ridley's play for teenagers, *Moonfleece*, was banned by Dudley Council. It was a play that referenced racism, the far right and the BNP, so the only people it could have offended were BNP racists. They were suspected of putting pressure on the local council.

Phil is no stranger to controversy. In 2005 Faber refused to publish his play *Mercury Fur* because of its controversial subject matter and many critics also attacked it. I thought it was one of the greatest theatre experiences of my life, so I commissioned and directed Phil's next two plays, *Leaves of Glass* and *Piranha Heights*, the three plays forming a loose 'Brothers trilogy'. I asked Phil how the disturbing story of *Mercury Fur* had developed. He explained.

> 'I have never set out to shock. By that I mean I have never distorted the truth of the play – the truth of the characters in the play – to contrive a gratuitous moment purely for effect. In *Mercury Fur*, for example, I had no idea that it was going to lead to the torture and death of a child. It came out of the truth of what the play demanded. The play is about a gang who, in a dystopian near future where society had broken down, make their money by providing rich clients with their darkest fantasies. Now...what's

that 'darkest fantasy' to be? Sleeping with a prostitute? Some hard-core bondage? Drugs? Well, you don't need a dystopian near future to be able to do that. The stakes of the play, and what the gang were doing, would be almost ridiculously low if I chose something like that. I had to come up with something that could never normally happen and that would be morally repugnant to all. The worst thing I can imagine anyone wanting to do is harm a child. And so I had to make that the thing the client wanted and the gang had to provide. I had to be true to the emotional landscape of the world I was creating.'

Offending the mass audience

So how does TV compare? I asked Justin Young, writer and producer on family friendly *Holby City*, how compliance works at the BBC on a purely practical level.

'I think you have to have an awareness of who your audience is. The show I'm running at the moment is a mainstream BBC1 audience and so I write with an awareness that there are certain areas or subjects which would alienate them. That said, we have to be challenging, and I'm always keen for our storytelling to be bold without being provocative for the sake of it. There are clear absolutes for a show like this – people watch us because they want to invest in what is basically a moral world – ultimately our heroes are good and bad deeds ultimately will be punished. And the BBC carries certain expectations that are very different to those you'd get on, say, Channel 4. But within this, I make sure that all of our characters are morally complex and that there are sufficient shades of grey. On a practical level, BBC Compliance means that all of us in management positions are trained on courses to make us aware of our responsibilities. Every episode is scrutinised for possible subject matter or scenes which might cause offence. If there are grey areas, we will refer them to the Editorial Policy department who we work with closely to ensure that we are fulfilling our obligation to the BBC license payer to tell stories with sensitivity that are appropriate to the timeslot we're broadcasting in. If we're running a controversial story – for instance a recent paedophilia story – we'll consult with Ed Pol throughout the development process so that we can write it with a clear idea of what is acceptable and appropriate.'

I wondered how these mechanisms were experienced by TV writers working on politically controversial subjects. Novelist and screenwriter Ronan Bennett has covered many such themes in his work, his most recent TV drama being the superb *Top Boy*. I asked him whether he had experienced covert or overt censorship or whether he self-censored because he understood the system. I found his answer encouraging:

> 'I have never experienced any kind of censorship. On the contrary, producers and drama commissioners have positively encouraged me to write what is important to me. I would similarly encourage emerging writers to follow their own instincts, loyalties and obsessions and not to try to second guess what audiences or commissioners want. That way lies hack work and failure. Stay true to what you want to say and say it brilliantly if you can.'

Ronan went on to explain how there were calls from Ulster Unionist David Trimble to ban *Love Lies Bleeding* (1993) and *Rebel Heart* (2001) but those calls were ignored by the BBC. He had a similar positive experience with *The Hamburg Cell* (2004, Channel 4) and *10 Days to War* (2008, BBC) in that he was supported throughout the process.

> 'You raise an interesting point about self-censorship. There is of course a lot in this. I would say that whatever I write, my starting point is that my first responsibility is to the film, to make the film work, to make it work as a film or drama. I would be quite happy to give the audience a sermon – as William Styron once said – but the problem for the putative sermon giver is that audiences and readers just don't want to listen to someone telling them what to

think. They want story, character, atmosphere, insight, the creation of a fully working, convincing fictional world. To the extent that I self-censor, it is with this in mind. Frankly, personally, I think the invasion of Iraq in 2003 without legal or moral justification. I marched against the war and I wrote newspaper articles attacking the Blair government's decision to join forces with Bush. But when it came to writing *10 Days to War* I couldn't write only from that point of view. Drama is not polemic. Drama needs conflict, difference, variation, light and shade. But cumulatively I would like to think the *10 Days* films added to the anti-war case. I hope so.'

In the UK we have many means at our disposal – political, legal and cultural – to protect the pure artistic expression of a work. However, unless, as in Ronan's positive experience, the protection of artistic integrity and free speech is the absolute value behind our strategies, those who start by championing the work can be driven by fear to silence it. Free speech is a contested right so we have a responsibility to fight for it. We need to continually push against the boundaries of what is deemed 'acceptable' or we will find those boundaries ever more conservatively drawn.

RULE BREAKER 29

Offend those who oppose freedom

RULE 30

Stay within the law

The legal obligations of a writer cover everything from avoiding copyright characters, depiction of real characters without permission to outright plagiarism or ensuring that enforceable contracts are in place before you start working with someone.

In the UK, health and safety legislation is frequently evoked (as in the case of *Behzti*). I am all in favour of protecting working conditions and public safety so it's interesting to think about how health and safety rules are used to justify containing dissent and also how they are viewed by artists beyond the UK as a lack of freedom.[25] Visiting Iran in 2010, I experienced the sort of censorship you might expect from a sadistic theocracy that advocates gender apartheid. As you will know Iranian writer/ directors have nonetheless created some of the most beautiful films in the world today. Anyhow, by contrast, health and safety regulations in Iranian theatre are lax. Iranian theatre makers who come to the UK bemoan our 'heavy censorship' in this area, saying that it's harder to create free theatre here than in Iran! I heard the same from Chinese Live Artists in relation to work in public places in the UK. Clearly a case of the devil you know, but fascinating from a British perspective. As with all laws, we should question who is being protected from what and why?

Live Artist Kim Noble explains how the needs of the artistic process when making *Kim Noble Will Die* overrode any legal consideration.

> 'I realise in today's desensitised world it's sometimes imperative (I've never used the word imperative before so I'm thankful for this opportunity) to up the 'stakes'

somehow. One part of a recent show necessitated the filming of me putting specimen jars of my ejaculate into supermarkets around the world and Peckham. My intention here isn't a need to break the law for an end in itself. Rather, the presenting of more unusual and subversive matter to engage and challenge the audience, this specific filming and action just happened to be 'against the law'.

I have a huge fear of the police and incarceration. So it's not something I relish. Perhaps on some subconscious level I'm breaking my own rules. Not ones that exist out in the art/theatre world but ones inside of me. Challenging my own fears. I was driven to do this. An interviewer once accompanied me on a particular hidden camera injunction in a shop and it was only later that he commented on the rush, the sheer panic he felt in being witness to this guerrilla tactic. It was only after that interview and through the eyes of someone else I become aware of the 'rule breaking' and its potential consequences.'

In an overtly repressive society you are unlikely to break the law so innocently, the act will be more consciously political. In Iran, land of double-think, it seemed impossible for artists to do anything meaningful without bending or breaking the rules. Being true to your art there could mean risking imprisonment, torture or death. As I write this, one of the world's greatest film-makers, Jafar Panahi, is still under house arrest and has been forbidden to make films for twenty years. When we met in Iran early in 2010, he had already been taken in for interrogation during which he was accused of the thought-crime of imagining a film about the post-election demonstrations. His witty response to the interrogator was, 'I don't know what kind of film I will make in the future. But now you are in my consciousness, maybe you'll even be in the film. I wonder how you'll end up – a hero or a villain?'

As Jafar Panahi indicates, repression of stories only gives birth to new ones. Though people may be silenced, the imagination can't be stopped. When creative freedom is threatened, so is the future of humanity. For every Panahi that is incarcerated, another hundred artists will be born.

RULE BREAKER 30

When the law is unjust, break it

RULE 31

'The purpose of art is not to change but to delight'

David Mamet, *Three Uses of the Knife* [26]

When you have finished a great story as a writer, reader or audience member you are a different person to when you began, you experience the world in a new way. So why Mamet's assertion? Well he suggests that if you set out to change an audience's feelings about an injustice, you are assuming a moral superiority over that audience. Your supposed 'enlightenment' is equally oppressive to the injustice that it sets out to challenge.

A cousin of this rule is 'Don't preach to the converted'. Oladipo Agboluaje wrote a play about a preacher that was delightful *and* revolutionary. He takes issue with Mamet.

> 'I don't see why art can't do both. As a purpose, I don't see my work as the next *Bible*. But I do fantasize of my work as being capable of moving people to make the world a better place by looking at their lives in a different light. It is a fantasy that keeps me challenging myself and making me think of how to write the next play better. In *The Christ of Coldharbour Lane*, the lead character literally wants to change the world by trying to change people. Even with its apocalyptic ending there is still hope that a new and better world is coming. It is a brutal satire that provokes laughter and outrage. I love to think of how the world can be a better place in a world where human beings are unchanging. Art can cause shock and outrage

as much as it can cause delight – Ibsen's *A Doll's House* for instance.'

I agree that Mamet's dichotomy is false. Of course we're uplifted by great theatre – a process of transcendence. Like Mamet, I've witnessed my share of dull, worthy, instrumental art which purports to change. I've also experienced boring, formalist, narcissistic art which purports to delight. Both extremes negate art. Bad art can exist for all sorts of good reasons. Bad theatre, which Mamet refers to here, always seems worse, to those of us who love it, than any other badly executed form.

Theatre is live and ever changing. As spectators we watch real people playing out the lives of others, facing choices and acting upon them. Through the process of empathy, we test out our own ethical framework (**Rule 13**). In Boal's forum theatre, we get up and make these choices as 'spect-actors'. On the streets, we witness/join art activists pitted against true-life antagonists in real time and space. Having worked as an artist across this spectrum of forms, and at many points in between, I know that theatre can genuinely transform people to see the world differently. For example *The Bogus Woman* by Kay Adshead is an impassioned cry against a terrible political injustice on behalf of people who have no voice in our society. Kay is a remarkable poet and her partiality feels the most powerful choice. When we first performed the play, audiences were horrified by the revelations and in post-show conversations it became clear that prejudiced perspectives towards asylum seekers had been changed through empathy.

Creativity grows from an unconscious, irrational impulse and politics from a more conscious, rational impulse. Ideas percolate slowly through your psychological, physical being, until they emerge organically. This freedom of the inner life, this optimistic openness to the world, must then be consciously critiqued. You are the skeptical eye on your vision, pulling the rug from under yourself, challenging your original perspective. Ronan Bennett touches on this in **Rule 29** when he talks about avoiding sermons. You are changed by this writing journey. Change also occurs in the imagination of your audience-reader. As a writer, if you're not seeking transformation, if you don't want to add to the world the choice of something other than what exists, then why write at all?

Many writers instinctively feel that our hopes for the future lie with the imagination, but this is a lawless zone fiercely fought for. All work is inscribed with values – either the values of our present system, or values which challenge those 'common sense' assumptions and engage critically with our society. 'Political' has become a euphemism for the art of change, though work which shores up the status quo is equally political. In this sense, 'preaching to the converted' is less true of oppositional work than it is of work which reinforces the majority view.

It is theatre's quality of nowness that re-sensitises us to ourselves and to the world, making it a barometer of our times. But drama lives beyond the moment and it is the mature political visions that we revisit most – plays about power by writers such as Euripides, Shakespeare, Ibsen, Brecht, Genet. Through great writing we explore our humanity and precisely our inspiring human potential to imagine and create change.

RULE BREAKER 31

The purpose of art is to change, not simply to delight

RULES 32-36

The Etiquette of Rewriting and Feedback

'An intellectual says a simple thing in a hard way. An artist says a hard thing in a simple way'

Charles Bukowski

RULE 32

Writing is rewriting

I rewrite a lot, over and over again, so that it looks like I never did.

Toni Morrison[27]

You got there, made it to the end of your first draft. Well done! That's amazing. Wow! You feel on top of the world – a sense of complete release. This euphoria might last for an hour, a day, a week. If you can, have a break from your finished draft for a fortnight at least. This isn't your reward by the way, though I hope you will celebrate your achievement. It's simply that you need to put space between yourself and the work to see it clearly. Sometimes, a deadline makes this impossible and you're more reliant upon the fresh eyes of others.

Every writer approaches the build up to the rewrite instinctively. When you return to your draft, try rereading it a few times in different ways. This first read tells you most, because of the distance you have put between yourself and the script. You might first try reading as if it wasn't yours, as if you had chosen to read it for pleasure, quickly without making notes. Get a sense of how it works as a whole and your overall feeling towards it. How much you enjoy it or hate it can come as quite a shock. It can be tempting to jot down strong feelings as you reread, but try to resist and stay with the flow, or make notes sparingly. Better still, wait until you take a natural break from reading. Afterwards, in your own time, write down your impressions of the whole, your major concerns as well as what you enjoyed. Or just live with it all for a while, feeling that world again. On the next read, make notes if it helps you. When you reread a third time you might work towards line by line detail. Or you may only want to reread once and simply imagine, until you've found the path. Or you may want to imagine and not reread at all for a while.

Whatever your process, at some point you need to write down or simply consider all the big questions you have. Perhaps get inspired by some of the questions listed later in this section. When you've considered the areas you want to address and you feel clear about your approach, decide on your priorities. Don't dive in until you're ready and don't try to tackle everything at once. Choose your battles. Work on one element at a time as far as possible. Always deal with the biggest issues first. If you're not ready to attack the major question head on, play with options away from the manuscript, keep mulling and opening out its potential. There's no point tweaking a bit of dialogue, if the story structure isn't sound; no use finessing a character detail if the character is no longer needed.

I've met writers who swear that rewriting is the best bit, where you can be really creative. I can see the truth of this but for me nothing quite beats the thrill of writing the first draft. Rewriting always takes longer than you imagine and generally much longer than the writing itself. Funny that it takes less time to create a whole new world than to cut, amend and polish that world. If writing is seeing the magic unfold, rewriting is being the magician.

Embarking on your rewrite

Outside of your world, you enter it again with trepidation. What if you can't fully inhabit it? What if you can no longer see, and you mess it up? Writing *is* rewriting in the sense that the rewriting period is make or break and you feel that with one misstep, everything that went before might as well never have existed. That isn't true, of course, just a feeling.

Laura Bridgeman, novelist and playwright, explains the pitfalls:

> 'Occasionally you can try and over-edit, or panic about the work as you get onto the point of redrafting. This is a dangerous time, when you know the material so well that you can stop seeing the good in it. You start to tamper, or overcomplicate, or over explain.'

At the start of the rewriting process you're probably trying to create the best first draft for whatever context you're working towards – whether that's an unsolicited submission or a commission with an imminent deadline. Professionally, a 'first draft' means that you're ready to show it, that the quality of the writing and its story and originality of voice shine enough to persuade someone to take it forward to the next draft. It's nothing to do with how much work it took you to get there. You might have reworked your first draft five times before sending it out as a first draft. It can be hard to decide whether your work is ready to submit. When in doubt, take a break and don't rewrite while it's feeling stale. Test the water with a few submissions at a time.

Can writing and rewriting happen at once?

Most writers don't look back during the rough first draft, because it can kill the momentum. TV writer Lisa Holdsworth explains:

> 'The best advice I was ever given was to write your first draft as if you will be the only person who will ever see it. Because, in reality, you will be the only person who sees that draft. Just write and write until you get to the end. Don't worry about layout and spelling and grammar and overwriting. Leave yourself enough time to fix all that later because your first draft should be about story and character and dialogue and nothing else.'

Scrutinising what isn't working is what initiates rewrites and that's a very different impulse to writing. Some writers like to rewrite a bit during the first burst of story creation, editing the previous day's writing as a kind of warm-up to re-entering the world and creating the next few pages of story. This can also be a helpful tactic when there's a big scene you're avoiding though it may be better to skip it and return later in order to keep the creative momentum going. Some writers try to get the beginning right before continuing but this can create more problems than it solves, as screenwriter Steve Bailie points out:

> 'Don't self-censor, don't keep going back over what you've already written unnecessarily. You know what's working and what's not and you can fix that later. It's a whole lot easier to make a story work once you have a complete draft, however fast and loose it may be. Act One problems you frequently won't find a solution to until you get to the final act; but unless you move away from those Act One problems and keep going forward, you won't find the answers.'

Some questions to ask of a first draft

When you reread your manuscript, the questions you ask of it will be specific. However, detailed questions will also emerge through asking about generalities. The questions below are to assist you in assessing your first draft. Some questions will seem to apply to your story or medium, others won't, so just use or ignore as useful. Try not to let yourself off the hook, but if the parameters implied by some of the questions irritate or overwhelm you, then deal with them gradually or set them aside and find another way to address your rewrite. If you find the list helpful, the discussions and suggestions contained in the rest of the book will support you in working through these questions alongside your own.

- Have you chosen the right medium to tell this story? The right genre(s) or devices? Is your voice consistent to itself, however subversive the formal style/aesthetic?
- Is the world of the story believable? Does the audience-reader experience the environment in the right amount of detail? How can you enhance your fictional world?

- What is compelling about the premise and how might you deepen that?
- Does your story raise enough meaningful questions to keep the audience-reader hooked from moment to moment?
- Where are you being too ambitious or not ambitious enough?
- Are you clear about whose story you are telling?
- Does the chosen narrative/character point of view work and are the transitions between points of view clear?
- What changes from the beginning of the story to the end? For the world? For your main character(s)? For the audience-reader?
- Does the story take too long to get going? Does it signpost its direction too quickly?
- Does the story go to the end of the line? Does it end in the right place? Does it resolve, leave things open or a mix of the two? Are there false or multiple endings piling up? Does it leave the audience-reader where you want them to be?
- Are there any scenes, characters, actions, dialogue, descriptions that do nothing to help the story move forward? What is holding back the forward momentum of the story? For example, extraneous exposition, a memory, an obsession, a stuck character? What do they add and is it necessary? What will you lose/gain by cutting them?
- Is your control over the action too tight? Can it breathe? Are you allowing your characters the freedom to express themselves?
- Will the audience-reader empathise with your main character? Which part of their struggle is most empathic? Will the audience-reader care about other characters and your story? Why should they care in story terms? Are you convinced?

- Are the forces of antagonism strong enough to force your main character(s) to risk what means most to them? Have you tested your character(s) enough? Have you given your main character enough tough moral choices?
- Have you chosen the right amount of characters for the scale of the work/depth of the story?
- Is the story told in the best order? Are the scenes? Chapters? What would playing with chronology of any part do to the whole?
- Are the major turning points clear? Are the smaller shifts clear? Is the relationship between the two true to itself? Do all the scenes turn and if not, are you clear about the effect that you want?
- Are there any missing story beats/emotional gaps? Have you tracked your characters' journeys to discover them? How can you fulfill these beats? What are the strongest 'unmasking' moments? Are they in the right place? Is there enough conflict between each character's inner need (wound) and their external want (mask)? Do your characters have enough contradiction to feel real and interesting whilst being clear enough to drive the story?
- What do we need to know more or less of? Where have you overestimated or underestimated your audience-reader? Is anything too 'on the nose' – lacking subtlety or subtext? Is anything so subtle or sketchy that it isn't reading clearly? (Feedback is particularly useful here.)
- What are the moments that make you squirm in a good way? Are there any moments that make you squirm in a bad way that could make you squirm in a good way?
- Does your story create clear and specific sensory pictures? What's the look and feel of the world – in terms of images or scenography, style or vision? Can you sharpen the sensory world?

- Is the relationship between narrative and dialogue working? Are character actions translated sufficiently into physical/visual storytelling – is there the right amount of dramatisation? Does the balance between showing and telling work?
- Have you chosen the best setting for the conflict of each scene? Is the action the strongest it can be? How might the scene be strengthened and made more resonant to the whole by changing the setting or action in relation to each other?
- Is the dialogue authentic to the world you've created and to each individual character? Is it surprising, arresting, illuminating, full of conflict and subtext?
- Have you given your scenes 'cliffhanger' endings, flourishes, motifs, gags or other strong 'transition' devices that captivate the audience-reader? Do the transitions have their own style and if so what does it signify?
- Where does use of language work best and where is it least successful? Where is the poetry of the work held? How are rhythm and silence used?
- Are there moments of self-indulgence or purple passages that can go? Do you need to sacrifice any well turned phrases and poetic moments for the greater good of the story?
- What are the relatives or ghosts of your script? How are you doing something original or breaking new ground?
- Where are the games in your script and who controls them? Can you expand on playfulness or primal pleasure?
- Where is the humour held and where is the tragedy? Could you be more intriguing or daring in your relationship between the two?
- What are the recurring motifs and images? What is the structural metaphor or architecture of images? How might

you orchestrate or deepen these for greater impact and meaning?

- What are you trying to say and does it need saying? Why did you write it and who do you think it is for? What relationship is envisaged with the audience or reader?
- If you had to change one unchangeable thing what would it be?
- Are there any challenging budget implications? Have you done the necessary research? Any concerns around authenticity or legal issues? Do you have any thoughts about casting if it's a drama or marketing ideas for a novel?

Through the process of rewriting, your craft and self-awareness improve and this prepares you for your next new writing surge. How do you know when the rewriting process is finished? Well I'm not convinced that plays, novels or freer forms of writing are ever finished really. You can go on forever and personally I'm a fan of quirks and flaws. I do think you need sympathetic feedback most at the beginning and when you're not far off the end.

RULE BREAKER 32

If writing is magic, rewriting is being a magician

RULE 33

Have family or friends read, before submitting professionally

Every reader makes their own meanings as they experience your work and through doing so they gain a sense of ownership. When the reader knows you well, but doesn't know your writing, their relationship to your work is more complex. Most writers have a trusted friend or family member, often a long suffering partner, to whom they show their work. At an early stage in your writing career or at an early stage of the piece you're working on, this may also be the only person who loves you enough to struggle through its inevitable flaws.

Your personal focus group may often feel closer to your natural audience than the professional editor/producer types who will read your submission. However, unless your friends or family are also writing professionals, they are unlikely to understand the notion of your rough draft being 'in-progress.' They may simply tell you how wonderful it is and how clever you are. They may complain that it isn't as good as the last book they read or film they saw and resent the fact that you've spent less time with them than usual for the sake of writing it. They may genuinely think they're helping you by telling you it's no good because they don't want to see you fail. Everyone close to you has an agenda on you, whether they're aware of it or not. This means they will also have an agenda on your writing, which may be about the fact that you even write at all.

It can go horribly wrong. I went through years of crippling writer's block because I couldn't find a way to process negative feedback from a friend and I came to believe that my writing was no good. Of course I kept scribbling but I couldn't work towards anything. They weren't wasted years, because I helped so many other writers along the way, got inspired by their writing and learnt to understand my own creative process better. I broke through my insecurity finally by completing the screenplay I had started writing ten years before. I then wrote *Hoxton Story*, a more collaborative piece, which used an element of my screenplay story.

Collaborative writing scenarios excepted, I believe it is inadvisable to show your work to anyone untested, until you're clear about why you are writing it and what it means to you. Only when you can't or don't want to continue without feedback, should you show it. Try to avoid sharing it to seek reassurance. The stronger your sense of the work, the easier it will be to listen and take on board feedback and to know whether or not you agree or disagree with it.

Never destroy a relationship for the sake of your writing. OK, never say never, it might be necessary, but try to find a way through. Remember that whilst it takes courage for you to share your scrawlings with those you love, it also takes time and patience for them to read and give you feedback. They are doing you a big favour. If you can keep your feelings out of it you may get some useful insights, but if your writing appears to have brought out the sadist in a gentle friend, don't pursue it. Wait for professional advice.

'Friendly' readers like to analyse you rather than your work. *Well I know where that bit came from! I remember that night!* (usually one you don't remember – probably because you weren't there); *That character was Pauline wasn't it? I don't think you quite got her though* (that's because the character is nothing like Pauline and wasn't intended to be).

Talking your work through on such terms can be asking for trouble if you're already feeling fragile. So if you must share with loved ones and close supporters, then give them specific questions – the ones below are simply to inspire your own – and ask them if they wouldn't mind *writing feedback down*. Then it's up to you to follow up.

> What does the title evoke for you?
>
> Did you find the world believable and consistent to itself? Anything you didn't believe?
>
> Where did you drift off and where did you want to read on and why?
>
> What elements of the story appealed to you and what didn't? Why?
>
> Did you find yourself wanting to know what happened to any particular character? Any characters you didn't engage with?
>
> What changed for the main character from the beginning to the end?
>
> Were there any moments that moved you or made you laugh?
>
> Where did you get most involved in the story and why?
>
> If you could add/take away one event or element to improve this story what would it be?
>
> How did you feel at the end?
>
> Was there anything that confused you or you didn't understand?
>
> Do you think you are the reader-audience for this work and if not who do you think it's for?

Another way to assess your work is to ask a friend (or a group of friends if it's drama) to read the work out loud for you without feeding back at all. Of course you should always read your own work out loud for yourself. It's not the same exercise as hearing it, but it can tell you where the issues are.

Different again is reading your work for others. Philip Ridley always reads the first draft of his plays aloud to me, playing all the roles. It feels very special. If you're confident enough, you might read your work to a friend to get a better sense of its story. Words live differently between people.

RULE BREAKER 33

Own your process.
Be careful who you share with.

RULE 34

Murder your darlings

Whenever you feel the impulse to perpetrate a piece of exceptionally fine writing, obey it – whole-heartedly – and delete it before sending your manuscript to press. Murder your darlings.

Arthur Quiller-Couch[28]

So this killer rule isn't about your feelings towards friends and family after they've given you feedback (**Rule 33**). Murder your darlings implies that your best loved bits of writing are the worst. M.J. Hyland touched on this in **Rule 23**. The sections you've sweated blood to perfect can feel overwrought. When you've loved writing a scene and got lost in it, the ease shines through and it's a pleasure to read. Don't get me wrong. Writers can work hard to create that sense of ease, but for some, unease can be the result. That's usually because you've driven out the spontanaeity and you're striving to impress. If your aim is to display your brilliance, as Quiller notes above, you will always achieve the opposite effect. This is true of any art form.

Murder your darlings can also refer to those occasions when you have to sacrifice the part for the sake of the whole – your favourite scene, a well-turned phrase or a lovely poetic moment. Rule breakers might argue that we are too impatient, that we should revel more in the tangential path or the pleasures of language. You can also save your darlings and massacre the entire story.

In a broader sense this rule is simply about rigorous editing. In theatre we have the advantage of seeing a script on its feet in rehearsal and it's generally clear to a writer why half a page needs cutting. In TV and film, the choice may be taken away from you on the shoot, in the edit or often long before. If you're a novelist, well, you need fine instincts, but your advantage is that most people read novels, so even if you don't have an editor, a friend may help by reading some for you. Also when your novel does reach edit stage, you're unlikely to hear ten different opinions, as you might in TV, film or theatre.

'If you tell me to murder my darlings,' a writer friend told a producer, 'then I'll come and kill your children too.' Writing is an act of love, respect it. There is always a danger of over-editing. If you cut your story to the bone, you may find that it is no longer your story. So always picture the scene as you consider a cut, live through it again, feel the rhythm, tempo and emotional pulse. Then read it aloud. That's the best way to avoid wrongful executions.

See other rules for further guidance on economy: **Keep your language fresh, original and vivid (Rule 23); Less is more (Rule 25); Show don't tell (Rule 26); Writing is rewriting (Rule 32)**.

RULE BREAKER 34

Don't be a hanging judge – avoid wrongful executions

RULE 35

Never argue with feedback

Getting professional feedback can be an invaluable, validating experience, shining a spotlight on what works and what doesn't. However, it's hard to respond to feedback that doesn't resonate with your gut instinct. You might not trust the criticism, but sometimes you're just not ready to hear it. How do you know the difference?

The honest answer is that you can only know when you know. If the unwelcome feedback is coming from someone whose opinions you generally respect, who has been helpful in the past, then definitely keep their ideas in the mix. The likelihood is that their critique is valid and you just can't see it yet. On the other hand, if this piece of feedback alone stops you trusting anything else the person says, then simply smile and say, 'Interesting! I'll think about that,' and move the discussion on.

If you trust the person generally but you don't agree with their point, then you might want to probe it further through open questioning, tease out their perspective. *What is lacking for you there? What do you want more of?* Sometimes, it can be helpful to get stuck in and work through their 'wrong' idea. Also, if the comments you're getting are bad, half-formed or poorly expressed, consider whether they might be pointing to a deeper truth or a really good idea. *Is that the kind of thing you mean?*

Try to be patient. Commissioners and editors sometimes give the impression that they have secret rules to follow but all they know is what doesn't work for them. Sometimes they might indicate a solution and their ideas can be gold dust, but finally it's your job to solve the story, not theirs. They can never know better than you what to write, so if time allows and you feel confused, get a second opinion or take a break before you dive into a decisive rewrite.

Don't expect the gatekeepers to know your work as well as you do. They are there to help you, but they may not be able to for any number of reasons, including not having read your work closely or sensitively enough. Their take will also be defined by their role in the process. An executive producer has different priorities to a director or an editor. You can learn something from anyone. It's up to you to glean all you can from a meeting (or emailed notes, letter or report) and to sift through what is useful and what isn't. If a notes session is going well or badly, it can be as much down to you asking the right questions and pursuing your agenda, as it is about the approach of the person giving you feedback.

Accept feedback with good grace unless it's abusive (see below). Only view unwelcome feedback as interference when the fee or future production is at stake. Otherwise it's just an opinion to take or leave. If you're not under commission, you should be particularly grateful to someone who has made time to help you. Most new writers recognise the support that enables them to take their work to the next level, but a few can be self-serving. Be gracious. People who offer to help you improve are making an emotional investment.

Take effusive praise with a pinch of salt when it's coming from someone who doesn't make the decision about your project. There are people paid to love everything you deliver, at least to your face. The recession is the latest in the line of 'I love it but our hands are tied' excuses for not commissioning, and of course it is often true. You must also ignore unmitigated condemnation.

Writer Rob Young got lucky and unlucky in swift succession when he was encouraged to adapt one of his delightful, quirky theatre monologues into a film. The lucky bit was that it starred John Simm, Christina Ricci and John Hurt. The unlucky bit was that its final resemblance to the original play was simply the title, *Miranda* (2002). This was Rob's first experience of feedback in film.

'As a nervous, first-time writer, I entered the UK Film Council with trepidation. They had agreed to invest £1m into my film but with a caveat, notes. So, the producers and I sat down to hear the notes of an expert. He began the meeting like this, 'I hate every single thing about this script, I absolutely hate it. The only reason I am in this meeting is because my boss is making me be here'. He then sniggered like a naughty schoolboy. His proactive solution was that the film should open with the lead character reading a book entitled, *How To Write A Terrible Screenplay* to inform the audience that the entire movie was 'meant to be crap'. As notes go, that was a tough one. And this was the man looking after my baby. He spent the next year doing all he could to bury the film. What started off as my promising project was mauled by various uncredited writers and 72 drafts later, was a flop.'

Unless you're on an urgent time frame with last-minute rewrites, your tendency may be to avoid argument. Rob's nightmare experience confirms that keeping the art is more important than keeping the peace. Differences between artists are generally creative spurs to new ideas, but that isn't always the case with non-artistic collaborators. If your colleagues are insisting on something that you know won't work, then put your case in the most polite, persuasive way possible. Seasoned screenwriter Terry Hodgkinson says:

'There are story editors out there in film and TV land who don't have a single creative bone in their bodies. Sure, they can move the structure around, and make scenes shorter, in the house style, but when they insist on inserting their own dialogue and characters into your script, beware! If your style is of the John Le Carré school, then their sad Enid Blyton lines are simply not going to fit no matter how hard you try. When it's transmitted, their crap dialogue will stand out a mile, and don't forget your name goes up front. It's so easy, with comparatively big fees involved for both first time and established writers, to accept it. In the feet planted firmly on the ground department, when you think of the cheque dropping on the mat, it's much less of a hassle to just say, 'I agree. You're right. Why didn't I think of that?' Don't be a prima donna, but don't give in to them without putting up a fight. Argue your creative case without flying off the handle. After all, you're the script writer, that's why they hired you. It's your work not theirs, you painted the picture. But if it gets to the point where the story editor wants to change your story beyond all recognition, consider carefully what you want to do. Magnolia emulsion or the Sistine Chapel?'

If you fundamentally disagree with the feedback from your editor, director, publisher or producer and things have reached an impasse, then you need to negotiate some kind of compromise. Otherwise you face being sacked, which happens a lot in TV and film, or walking away from your project and/or removing your name. That can be a tough call. On the one hand, you don't want your name on a turkey, but neither do you want to lose the project altogether.

It is typically the ticking clock that creates such tensions, rather than the good intentions of your collaborators. There are exceptions, as above, but usually everyone wants your work to be as successful as you do, even if their ideas of how to get there differ from your own. 'Scripted from devised' theatre shows, co-writing partnerships and much TV and film involve collaboration and are rarely about being an auteur. You need to be flexible and open to compromise, whilst standing up for the artistic integrity of your project. If this makes you feel unhappy or as if you're losing your identity, then you're probably better off choosing a more independent process or another medium. This might not pay the bills, but perhaps it's more important to look back on your writing life and feel proud of your choices.

RULE BREAKER 35

Accept the feedback that works for you

RULE 36

The rejection of your work isn't personal

The whole matter has been a great distress and worry to me, but I try to console myself by thinking it is only through undergoing all varieties of human experience however distressing some of them may be, that a writer can hope in the end perhaps to produce work of permanent value.

Somerset Maugham[29]

One of the greatest challenges for a writer is to be sensitive and open to the world in order to create and simultaneously be thick-skinned enough to take the knocks, some of which may be public. In what other job would you be expected to be quite so tough in the face of constant criticism, whilst remaining vulnerable in order to excel? You need to protect your creativity as you would protect a child. Who is protecting you?

Of course rejection isn't meant personally, but sometimes you feel it personally. Let's not pretend. You're not juggling figures, writing reports or making widgets. You're an artist with a layer of skin missing. How else did you get to imagine and share your unique vision of the world? I love the Somerset Maugham quote above in relation to this rule. I challenge you to use every painful experience, even that of having your writing trashed, to enhance and deepen your writing.

When no one seems to like it

The company or individual that has rejected your work isn't right for it. That can be hard to face but we all know that most successful writers were rejected many times before breaking through. Many successful writers still face rejection of their pitches or work, in spite of their good name. Resilience, persistence and a need to keep writing are the keys to success.

So keep living, observing life and creating new worlds. Find champions for your project who will promote it for you and/or give moral support; people who can coach you through, maybe a friend or agent or mentor who'll tell you how great some aspect of your writing is. *OK so it needs a rewrite but it's still great.*

If your project has been reworked enough, is truly on the skids and in spite of that you still have a passion for it, there are always options. Keep it for another time, find a way to self-produce/publish or alternatively see if there is any aspect of it that could be used as the beginning of a new project. This might be a character, a scene or a storyline. Mull it over. Return to it afresh.

If you can't see the funny side – yes sometimes there is one – at least try to maintain your dignity and self-belief. Bounce back into the world with a smile on your face. Use rejection to motivate your next project. If you feel badly under attack, withdraw a little rather than turn your open heart to stone. Protect your creative impulse from the cruel world. Start new projects but keep them to yourself for a while.

Public rejection

When your artistic work, your gift to others, finally gets through all these hurdles to production or publication, you should be able to enjoy the response of your reader-audience. But what if your work gets publicly debated as if it were some negative force in the world? That sweet story you gave all your love to for years is dismissed in reviews as worthless. Someone belittles you in a blog. Others agree. Even your friends change the subject. You wanted everyone to be touched by it. You feel bereft, misunderstood, defeated. This is a normal, human response, however fleeting and however robust your self-belief.

Just to really cheer you up, the flip side can also be true. If your work is highly acclaimed you can also lose perspective on what you're doing. Pity the poor writer whose first work is over-hyped. How do you keep going when you know that your next book or play will probably be damned? The 'second album syndrome' is a tough one for writers, particularly if everyone suddenly wants a piece of you. Try not to feel rushed if your first work has been a major hit, and resist the temptation of too many commissions. Set your own pace.

Trust your own judgement

The key to resilience is never to trust anyone's opinion of your work more than your own. This applies equally to praise and criticism. If you know your work is strong, then rejection may annoy you but it won't deeply wound. Writing is a subjective business and as this book tries to make clear, one steeped in conventions not of your making.

Some of the most original contributors to this book have faced sickening rejection, not because their work was worse than other people's but I believe, in some cases, because it was better. There are instances when you can take rejection as a kind of compliment.

In my experience...

In 1999 I was trying to produce *The Bogus Woman*, a new play about an asylum seeker at a time when little had been written about their situation in the UK. Kay Adshead's writing was astonishing but not a single theatre in London would touch it. It was a one-person play, and we had a brilliant but then unknown actress – Noma Dumezweni – playing over thirty roles. At one stage, even Kay's agent suggested that I was scuppering its chances by trying to take it forward as a one-person play because 'it needs at least five actors!' I suspect this was feedback she'd received.

Eventually the Traverse Theatre had something drop out and they offered to take it for ten performances as part of the Edinburgh Festival. The Arts Council agreed to fund it and the Bush Theatre said if it got rave reviews across the board and a Fringe First they would consider bringing it to London. The play did all this and was the hit of the Festival. It then went on to tour internationally and win other awards, selling out everywhere. The same play that everyone turned down became one of the most important shows of that year. It is still produced – sadly it is still as politically relevant today.

The arts world is no more a meritocracy than the world beyond it. You have to steel yourself for conservatism and cliqueness. If your offer is genuinely original (particularly if it's politically or formally subversive) chances are it will get multiple rejections. Always remember that the 'nos' don't count. You only need one 'yes'. Just keep on going until you get it. Somewhere out there is a visionary like you who can see around corners too.

RULE BREAKER 36

Rejection is personal, so use it to fuel your writing

RULES 37-40

Maxims of process and profession

There are many aspects to a writer's professional life. I will focus here on a few common maxims and discuss what lies behind and beyond them.

RULE 37

Ignore the saboteurs in your writing life

The worst enemy to creativity is self-doubt. Sylvia Plath

All creative work relies on an optimistic confidence of vision, a childlike belief in the endeavour, a freedom to be honest about whatever the hell you want. Judgement is vital, and distinct from self-doubt. Cutting 50% of your script is judgement. Sitting on the script for a fortnight and staring out of the window is uncertainty. Putting the flawed script away and telling yourself it's pointless, that's self-doubt.

We all have saboteur voices in our heads. They usually stem from someone else's negative opinion of our worth. The self-doubt may be triggered by a recent event, but its source is often childhood. Inevitably, these voices come from our own sense of inadequacy to the goal we've set ourselves. They may mask other insecurities – for example stuff like having no money, not being accepted or not feeling clever enough. Age, class, education and time to write are favourites in the low self-esteem stakes. Saboteur voices delight in other people's rejection, use it as evidence of how crap we are. *Six good reviews. OK. But what about the bad one?! He laughed at your idea, it must be shit. You're just stupid, so and so said so. What makes you think you can do that?!*

Sound familiar? Saboteur voices come and go. It's bloody hard to be a writer and then you beat yourself up too. Strong egos tend to triumph in the arts and the more fragile writers, who may have great talent, disappear from a particular writing scene, unable to defend themselves against the unrealistic demands of their 'industry'.

Saboteur voices can take sinister forms. Those voices that compel you to go against yourself, your true voice, because somehow your work will be more acceptable if it's more like whatever writer is flavour of the month. Those voices that say you must give in at a script meeting to some idiot who doesn't get your work because otherwise it won't go on, even though, to use Terry Hodgkinson's phrase in **Rule 35**, you know it's a magnolia paint job.

Then there are those voices that tell you there's no point getting up, you don't feel like writing today and anyway, no one will care if you do, no one will ever produce it so what's the point? Those voices that tell you that you will never have another thought worth committing to a piece of paper. Damn those voices.

Confront the saboteurs

Inside you these saboteur voices do battle with another set of voices – the voices of your characters in the world you have created for them. Yes, you did that, you! You created a whole world. In your imagination, on paper, in your body. How amazing is that? Your characters are strong enough to drown out the other voices; your characters are more real and they want to live their stories! Let them breathe again, your characters, they are waiting for you to bring them back to life. What are you waiting for? Go and play in their world.

You can only silence the saboteurs by writing. You can also turn your saboteurs into a creative spring. Most of the saboteurs in my life have inspired characters or interpretations in my work as a director/writer. Bullies and bastards take on a different life in fiction, but I always let them into my work and it's led to some dark and amusing choices. If you want to take revenge you can always kill them off, give them a walk on part or both!

Playwright Paula B. Stanic, winner of the 2008 Alfred Fagon Award, explains how she deals with her saboteur voices:

> 'I have to listen to get over them. Others may be able to ignore or block them out, I can't. I was stuck for months because of a comment made about my writing by someone at a theatre I had always wanted to work for. The comment I think was meant to point out something I could look at and fix, but it was actually a criticism that meant altering my style/voice. It stayed with me because I felt that it meant I would never work there unless I changed. For months I just tried to erase this comment from my head. It didn't work, every time I started to write anything it was there. It was when I listened and had a go at writing something in the way suggested, I knew it wasn't me. I hated what I came up with. I had to listen and do that to get past it.'

So prove your saboteur wrong. Remember, when you're writing, some people will disrespect you or give you the benefit of their ignorance. Many will sit on the fence. Then there are others, lovely others, who will support you. Focus on them.

Exercises for saboteur exorcism

List your achievements

List all the great things you would never have done if you'd listened to other people. Unless you're particularly fortunate, I'm sure that list includes every achievement of which you're most proud. I know mine does.

List your supporters

List all the positive things that anyone has ever said or done to help you take your writing forward. That teacher who encouraged you, that writer who inspired you, your friend who recommended a book, that cup of tea your partner made for you that magically appeared as you typed… Anything and everything. Write them all down. You'll be amazed how much your writing has going for it.

Write a rave review of your present project

OK, this is a bit of a controversial one, because who cares about the critics right? But hey it's fun so why not just enjoy cheering yourself up by saying all the great things your piece of work will become.

Write affirmations for action

Affirmations can be quick fixes or they can be positive prompts to action, as in this exercise. As you write what you feel you start to reconnect with your own passion and integrity. Feel free to make up your own prompts of course.

I love my character X because....

I need to tell this story because....

My voice is important because.....

Confronting self-limiting beliefs

I trained and practise as a coach. This is a well-known coaching exercise that I've adapted for writers. It can help you to confront and reframe self-limiting beliefs and use your saboteur voices to help rather than hinder you. Without a coach to support you, you will need to be very honest with yourself to do this exercise. Maybe find a friend and you can coach each other. Just keep gently probing, using only open questions. These are how, what, when questions that can't be answered with a yes or no. It's OK to keep returning to the same issue until you nail it effectively. You can do this six stage exercise with anything the saboteur voices say.

1. **Take the negative belief** that you or someone else holds about your writing. Write it down, e.g. 'I'm crap at structure'. You will know if it is a belief rather than the truth because you will probably phrase it as an absolute.

Phrases such as *I always; I never; I can't; it won't happen* may be implied, as in the above statement. They are not true, they are a belief you're holding onto for some reason, so let's explore that a bit.

2. **When did you first start to hold this belief?** Can you trace it to a particular event or period in your life? For example, 'the critical reaction to my first play,' or 'I had a chaotic childhood – my writing came out of chaos.' What happened there?

3. **What purpose does this belief serve?** What need has it served in the past? Can that need be met elsewhere? **Is the belief still relevant?** For example, 'I didn't go to university and I think that's why I'm crap at structure. But also I suppose deep down I associate creativity and chaos, I resist linear thinking. Rather than work on my craft I've been indulging an inferiority complex…' And so on.

4. **What is the impact of this belief on your writing? What might your writing be like if you didn't have this belief?** For example, 'It has become a self-fulfilling prophecy. I don't know how well structured my writing would be if I stopped sabotaging myself.'

5. **What's the evidence for this belief?** 'One awkwardly structured play.' **Can you counter it? Has there ever been a time…?** 'My kids know I'm good at telling stories.' **How could you reframe this into an empowering belief that supports your writing? What language might you choose?** Write it down, e.g., 'I'm an accomplished storyteller.'

6. **Challenge yourself to nurture/reinforce this new way of thinking.** Identify an action you can follow to enable that – a challenge to yourself. Make the action singular in

focus and try to state it as a pithy one liner if you can. For example, 'A story a day.' This writer decided to tell a bit of what she was working on in the form of a story a day to someone she cared for. She might change the character, setting etc., but she would focus on telling the story, with a beginning, a middle and an end. No doubt she was already telling stories many times a day as we all do! It was her new awareness of this and linking it to her working process that she chose to consciously develop.

Don't go mad

I started this rule with a quote from Sylvia Plath. We can all cite high-profile cases of mentally ill or suicidal writers. There is some evidence of a link between creativity and certain mood disorders. Writers look at our crazy world more closely and honestly than most people but many would also assert that their creativity saves them from madness. Whether mental illness is more or less prevalent in writers than the rest of the population is a moot point. If it's happening to you and you are a writer, inevitably it will feel connected to your writing. After all, you work through your imagination, so you are constantly moving between rational and irrational thought.

Mental illness can affect everyone and it is often completely beyond your control. However, the following experiences have tipped writer friends of mine temporarily over the edge and you can learn to recognise warning signs in yourself.

- The patterns that you see, the connections that you make in terms of ideas or images, take on a life of their own that goes beyond the ordinary transformational writing experience into a form of psychosis.
- You fall into a deep depression where you feel unable to write, possibly precipitated by a sense of failure connected to your writing.

- You compare your own achievements to those of others. You define your success by external measures rather than intrinsic values. Paranoia kicks in.
- You are writing furiously to the point where you stop eating or sleeping and tip over into a hypomanic state.
- You start using alcohol or drugs to write or escape from writing and it becomes an addiction.
- Your neuroses or ritual behaviours develop into extreme phobias and obsessions that incapacitate your professional life.

You can avoid some of the above tipping points by being self-aware and living a healthy life with emotional support from empathetic people who can offer a more objective outlook. Mental illness is no fun to experience or to be around. On the other hand, going out and having fun may be just what you need to relax and get perspective. As a writer you have already taken value-driven choices and are in a better place than most people to integrate your deepest vision with your life and be clear about your goals. That is your life's work in every sense and the strongest basis there is for mental health and happiness.

Whatever helps get you through, the problem with this rule is that by denying your saboteurs, you may sabotage yourself further. Confront them, use them up, live with them. Then let them go.

RULE BREAKER 37

Confront the saboteurs in your writing life

RULE 38

Learn how to be alone

Being alone is wonderful. It is liberating. You're not alone of course. The world of your imagination is exciting, seething with lives that completely absorb you. It's compulsive living with people who fascinate you and can't hurt you. Your characters, I mean!

Solitude is vital to most kinds of writing. So is peace. You need time to dream alone, to just walk or stare at the sky.

Finding time to be alone

Practically making time to write can be a challenge with demands like work or family. If you have to write however, you will find a way to do it. Here are a few time-creating suggestions.

- Put writing times in your diary, show up on time and don't let yourself down. You might start with half an hour in the morning, by getting up early with a couple of two-hour slots added on evenings and/or weekends. You will probably enjoy this so much that you will somehow, very quickly, find the extra hours a week you need to go beyond that warm-up.
- Only say yes to social engagements that you'll enjoy more than writing and you'll be astonished how quickly your diary clears. Limiting TV/internet etc. to two hours a week, unless it's research, will free a lot of time. Try disconnecting the internet while you write.
- Many writers with families get up very early or work very late to find quiet concentrated writing time when others are asleep.

- Develop the story in your mind whilst doing other things – this will happen naturally but you can also consciously choose to spend time with it.
- Sort out your work area/stationery/laptop etc so you will want to write as soon as you find a spare moment. Make sure your chair is comfortable and lighting is good. If you can't make a designated space don't worry. Always carry a notebook you like around with you. I started my current project, a novel, on the bus going to and from work.
- Use writing as a reward. When you've finished some work or chores treat yourself to the ten-minute story in **Rule 2** or an equivalent fun writing exercise.

Loneliness

Writing is a very different experience for those of you who already do it for a living and spend days or weeks alone. Sometimes your characters' dynamism deserts you. You are desperate to live in their world but writing is sluggish. Where did the muse go? On those days it can be tough to be alone – because now you truly are alone and you don't even have the excuse of no time. Playwright Paula B. Stanic tells me:

> 'I spoke to a writer just yesterday who said she had given up and started teaching because she realised she couldn't stand being alone. I really enjoy it. There's a kind of madness to it, that you're going into different worlds, and creating dilemmas, emotions and situations in your head, but I enjoy that. It's great having those first conversations with a company, theatre or director when you're starting out on an idea. Those discussions get you really fired up, but then at some point you just have to go away and get on with it. I've collaborated with other writers on two different pieces. One also involved collaborating with the actors and there was still a period where we had to go away and work by ourselves. It's just part of writing.'

I'm with Paula on this; I love the solitude of writing. However, I know that extrovert writers become uneasy spending a lot of time alone. The fast turnaround writing schedule doesn't work when there's no time for them to 'phone a friend'. If this is you, build lots of other interaction into your schedule. Activities such as teaching or running workshops or more collective art forms may be needed to keep you buoyant, rather than full-time writing.

Novel writing is the least mediated and the most solitary form, though ironically novelists are expected to do more on a publicity front than would generally be required of writers in other mediums. Perhaps outspoken introverts are best suited to writing novels.

You'll never write alone

Children's author Tom Palmer feels differently about this question. Others are there with him as he writes, they contribute to his work, including those who read it.

> 'I do not write alone. When I write a book I speak to at least ten people who know about things I don't know about. Soldiers who can tell me about military procedure. Football coaches help with training techniques. Fair trade farmers in Africa who tell me about how fair trade has changed their lives. As well as that, I show my book to at least ten people as I am writing it, before it reaches my editor: my wife, three members of my writing group, a teacher, a soldier (again) and children who I have met in schools. And others. As a result I hope that my books are accurate and filled with genuine detail. Yes, I make up a lot of it in my head on my own: but a huge proportion of it is done with other people.'

So enjoy writing alone but if you need support remember it's out there in the world that your book is from and for. Writers across all mediums have also created a strong DIY culture of self-organised support groups, physical and virtual. If there isn't a writers group near you, join one online and connect with people who've experienced what you're going through. In the UK, there is a healthy sensibility towards work in progress and a lot of sharing online and live. Readings, workshops, scratch performances are good platforms for trying out ideas and material.

Of course the last thing you might want to do is to spend your precious free time with other writers. Groups can become an addictive distraction. Terry Hodgkinson voices what a lot of writers privately feel.

> 'Don't hang around with other writers. The ones who have never done anything else with their lives are sad and boring and can be very pompous.'

RULE BREAKER 38

You never write alone

RULE 39

You can't teach talent

I've heard this said of actors, directors, painters, all manner of artists. It's a variation of the 'born not made' argument. It's true that we have natural aptitude and that who we are, our perception of the world, is based on a complex mixture of factors that render us unique. Our talent is based in this inimitability and by definition, originality cannot be taught.

Being talented is a lifelong process. Talent is about who you are, how you are in relation to the world, the way you see life. As you change and grow so does your talent, even if you can't write as often as you like. How much time writers have to daydream, let alone practice, is not equal; like so many things in life it comes down to access, in this case primarily the ability to buy time and the commitment to make time. The opportunity to practice your craft is undoubtedly a key factor in the development of your talent.

Neuroscience confirms that creativity is learnable and our self-perception is related to that. As we observe from watching children engrossed in play, intrinsic motivation is vital to creativity and may be part of our survival drive, enabling us to keep inventing and problem solving long after we have come to a solution (**Rule 8**). We also enjoy being creative and will make huge sacrifices for the pleasure of being 'in flow', of being absorbed in our own ingenuity. Most importantly, although we each learn in individual and random ways, creativity is always expansive. This is why creativity is at its most heightened at the intersection of cultures or crossing of boundaries. Motivation to be creative is easily destroyed if too few opportunities for curiosity exist or if too many obstacles are put in the way of risk and exploration.

We are naturally creative at an early age. From as far back as I can remember, I always had two or three stories on the go in my head. I never shared them verbally or wrote them down, they just grew there like long-running serials whenever I was alone. I loved playing with dolls or improvising imaginary worlds with friends, though of course we didn't call it that. Sometimes I'd make up stories for my younger sister – a soft-toy soap opera got repeat viewings. We all have a unique relationship to storytelling. What are your own memories of inventing other worlds as a child? How does it inform your relationship with storytelling now?

My perspective on **You Can't Teach Talent** is that we need to *un*learn as much as learn. Children have a lot to teach adults about creativity. When we play as children we fly in imaginative leaps, not closing off any possible direction, unconcerned how the results may be viewed, making up the rules collaboratively as we need them. My niece found dolls' clothes fiddly so she created the 'Naked Barbie Army'. Children don't self-censor, they are in the moment. There is always so much laughter and extremity.

At some stage in your creative development, anxiety creeps in and with it the justification of being good at what you're doing or of saying something meaningful or in the 'right way'. As a writer who has happily scribbled in secret, you start to show your work to other people, shyly at first. What was once simply play starts to become a craft to you or even paid employment and you're desperate to improve. If you were playing the piano, acting or painting, you wouldn't think twice about taking lessons. But there is something about writing, you feel that either you've got it or you haven't.

Screenwriter Chris Lunt believes in learning from the masters rather than teachers, reading and watching the best there has been. He doesn't believe writing can be taught, only practised.

'I was fortunate enough to never have a formal education in any form of writing beyond an 'O' level in English language. All my experience comes from being a fan of film and television, and having a clear understanding of what I liked and how I perceived it worked. I'd always wanted to be a writer from an early age, but I'd kept it secret, coming into the industry by accident, initially as a cameraman, then slowly stepping sideways when I thought no one was looking.

Before I worked in television and film I'd worked in a number of very different industries. It was natural to me to bring a mindset over from those early and formative careers. From engineering it was a work ethic. If you're a writer, you write. Every single day, for as long as you can, but never for less than eight hours. I start work at eight thirty, and don't stop till at least six. The only way you'll become a better writer is by writing, as much as you can.

From sales I brought the idea of building a network. Understanding the industry and knowing what production companies and broadcasters are doing what. What about the once successful company that's just produced a dud? How many writers are sending them ideas right now? I have a brilliant agent – but I rely on myself to get out there and find the work and make the connections. I spend two thirds of my time writing, and one third managing my network and looking for the next gig. Don't mither, but build those relationships. Asking specifically what people are looking for can be a big help.'

When I got my first paid writing commissions in my early twenties I remember feeling that my writing was getting worse. I never experienced script development – a few plays were professionally produced pretty much in rough draft form. I cringe now to think of that, though luckily they were kindly received. I set up the

Young Writers Programme at Soho Theatre in 2000 to offer what I'd like to have had as a young writer in terms of guidance. What I *had* been fortunate to get were paid opportunities to write and I learned a lot through seeing my work on stage.

We all need different levels of support to access our potential at whatever age we start writing. Some of you feel naturally confident, just want to be left alone to create and become absorbed in the flow of that. Others need encouragement to keep going.

Trevor Byrne is from a new generation of writers who partly attribute their success to training. In his case it resulted in a fantastic first novel, *Ghosts and Lightning*.

> 'I believe all beginning writers should consider a creative writing programme. There are many reasons to do so. True, no one can 'teach talent', but a good creative writing program can – and will – help the beginning writer reach his potential. At minimum, it will help the writer avoid repeating dispiriting mistakes and making unhelpful assumptions about his work. We hear that writing is necessarily a lonely endeavour, but it doesn't have to be, particularly at the outset. I began my first novel as an undergraduate and refined it during many workshops on an MPhil program. Donald Ray Pollock, now a rightly celebrated writer, recently graduated from the MFA program at Ohio State University in his fifties, after working for 32 years in a paper mill.
>
> Perhaps most importantly of all, in a world where time seems short, and the role of the creative, imaginative, empathetic mind is often trivialized, a creative writing programme helps validate the writer's serious-minded choice to write in the first place. Immediately the writer has a critical readership for his work and has entered into a contract with others with similar aims and ideas. The writer is taken seriously, and is more easily able to take himself seriously. The condescending remarks of those inquiring after the status of your 'masterpiece', or the

> hesitant, well-meant wishes of family members seem less
> difficult to bear and, in time, will disappear.'

I'm not sure that going on a writing course will make what you do feel any more real to those you love. That wasn't my experience when I trained as a director – though if you listen to actors, directing is a role that even many directors don't understand! I do agree with Trevor that the self-belief you build by going through training with others can give you more resilience to being trashed and a stronger sense of your own work.

I've run enough writing workshops to know that they can have a positive impact. I was over in Istanbul in 2010 and a woman ran up to me and started talking excitedly. She'd come to one of my writing workshops in Turkey six years before, simply out of curiosity. The play she started that day had now won a major playwriting prize. For her, one writing workshop had opened a door that changed her life.

There are writing tutors out there who will inspire you. Others won't chime with your writing or learning process. We all need different things from a workshop. Approach any major writing course with a sense of what you want from it and being open to what may come your way. Good writing tutors are honest about their likes and dislikes. They won't judge the quality of your work on the basis of their subjective taste, but of course empathic connection helps. Try to find tutors who know the industry. If you get a teacher who wants you to write in their voice, run a mile. However, passion and an idiosyncratic approach can definitely be worth paying for.

I have read some very accomplished scripts by playwrights from MFA programmes in the US. It is partly a question of cultural taste but I felt that many had the raw life polished out of them. I would hate to see a situation in the UK where doing a creative writing programme becomes the main way to get your novels and scripts published or produced. That is asking writers to pay for a place at the table.

Dennis Kelly says:

> 'I think something you discover yourself is understood and supports your work, whereas something told to you by someone else can be mysterious and limiting. I've never read a writing book or done a course: I've been on the odd workshop, some of which have been fantastic and invaluable, but usually they've come at it from a different angle, like performing (the best one I ever did was by Phelim McDermott and was an improvising workshop).'

We're back to where we started. Vision comes from lived experience and freeing your imagination, but the practice of craft is vital to developing your authentic voice. A creative writing course can help you on that journey and may also offer professional contacts. No writer should feel compelled to train but the best writers are curious and open to the world. This may or may not lead you to enter a formal learning environment.

RULE BREAKER 39

You can develop talent

RULE 40

Just Write

It's true. You will get better at it, the more you do it. It will also take over your life.

Write 1,000 words/10 pages a day?

OK, so this word/page count trick works for a lot of people. Maybe people who liked homework at school or who make lists of goals and tick them off when completed. Only kidding. For some it does make writing easier and for others it's part of the job. Try it for yourself. Not talk about writing, think about writing, avoid writing but actually sit (or stand or lie down) and just write. Steve Bailie offers a professional perspective:

> 'If you want to make a living in television, you need to be not only good – but fast. That means treating writing like a proper job – full-time, every day, putting in overtime if you need to. Average turnaround time for a one-hour series drama script is 12 weeks, start to finish, from initial idea to shooting script. That'll take in at least 5 or 6 drafts, and you may have as little as 10 days in which to write the first draft. Writing is like going to the gym; the more you do it, the stronger you get. Stop for too long & it takes you a while to get up to speed again. The simple, single thing that characterises a real, working writer is that at the end of every work day they *will* have generated new pages. Some days it's one page, some days it's double figures. If I'm hitting ten pages a day on a first draft I know I'm well on track.'

But what if it's a speculative novel? Isn't writing 1,000 words of drivel a day pretty pointless? I hear you rebels. The good girls and boys say you need to write through these moments of doubt and your writing will improve. I get the psychology of that and I think it may be good advice for many, but if the muse takes a day off, personally I prefer to do the same; daydream, read, watch a movie, take a walk or better still go out and get a life. See friends. Those people you used to enjoy when you weren't writing on top of a full-time job. Remember them? There's nothing like depriving yourself of writing to make you hungry for it. Life itself creates the appetite to write. If you're a full-time writer up against a deadline, you won't have that luxury of time. 100 lines for you. Except there are no rules in this book.

Making clear, achievable, writing goals for each session is a more flexible solution to the feeling of being overwhelmed by a huge project. It might be word count or it could be 'I'm going to finish the swimming pool scene today'. It just depends. The question about self-discipline is apposite, but that often comes down to what's driving you to write, something we explored at the beginning of this book. On a daily level it's usually the meaning of a specific project that keeps you going. Great writers are driven as often to the desk by the need to feed the family as for some higher purpose. Even then, the material imperative is usually underpinned by another existential need. Writers who become rich rarely give up writing because of it. They were driven from the outset, they persisted for a reason and seldom was it fame or fortune.

Know what drives you

When we read or watch a writer's work, we search out the hidden meaning, the personal subtext, the world view. We feel an intimacy with the writer, even if the work repels us. Only if it bores us do we stop looking for the patterns and drift into a more interesting inner world of our own. If your writing is going to satisfy an audience, it has to satisfy your own desire too. If your heart's not in it, what's the point? Ronan Bennett tells me:

'I have a convention of my own that I never break and that is to write only what is important and personal to me. *Love Lies Bleeding, Face, The Hamburg Cell, Rebel Heart, Public Enemies, Hidden, Top Boy*, I had a deep connection with the characters and subject matter on all of these. They were felt, emotionally as well as intellectually.'

This question of subject and meaning and drive to write is personal and specific to each piece of writing but it's also social and political, it's about your connection as a writer to the world.

Consider for a moment your own drive to create...

> What do you want from this writing?
> What is your dream for it?
> How are you connecting with the changing world?
> What are you committed to?
> What is the world telling you?
> What is your heart telling you?

Here are some instinctive responses from writers participating in my workshops.

to tell a story that no one has heard before
to feel alive
to keep me sane
to escape into a different world
to open people's hearts
to express myself – if people want to they can share it
to remind people of something they've forgotten or take for granted
to collaborate with others
to provoke a reaction and change people's minds

Living as a writer will mean something different to each of you; for Tanika Gupta it is an unruly act of imagination that draws from and spills out into reality.

'Being a writer gives you license to be a little bit strange and to break the rules. Lying, ear wigging into conversations, getting obsessed with the darker side of human characteristics, digging into people's lives, psychoanalysing people, entertaining people, making them laugh, making them cry, 'ripping off scabs' as I like to say is all part and parcel of making a script work. You have to break social rules and not be afraid of offending anyone. I am strangely elated when I see my audiences trembling, disturbed or even weeping after one of my plays.'

As Tanika suggests, breaking rules is not just about how you write but how you live as a writer in the world, resisting its illusions through the power of your imagination, creating rules that enable freedom.

Eternally unfinished aspects

I started this book with a quote from Albert Camus. In his brilliant lecture 'Create Dangerously' (1957), he sums up the artist's dilemma:

'Art is neither complete rejection nor complete acceptance of what is. It is simultaneously rejection and acceptance, and this is why it must be a perpetually renewed wrenching apart. The artist constantly lives in such a state of ambiguity, incapable of negating the real and yet eternally bound to question it in its eternally unfinished aspects.'

RULE BREAKER 40

Don't just write, participate in the world

~~10~~ 11 Rules *for rule breakers*

1. Recognise your own rules - and overturn them
2. Break rules to be yourself - trust your gut instinct
   your vision, your heart
3. Do the opposite - if it's polished, scratch it
4. Be exacting in everything & certain of nothing
5. Have a good character do a bad thing,
   or a bad character do a good thing
6. Be curious, open and free
7. Do what seems wrong when it feels right
8. Be braver than the next person
9. Take power for more rule breaking - If you
   break rules you might only hold power for
   a short time, so break a lot
10. Free your imagination and destabilise
    the status quo
11. Practise the rules before you break them

P.S. Feel free to break and add
your own!

Notes

1   Albert Camus, (1975; 1942), 'The Absurd Man' in *The Myth of Sisyphus*, London: Penguin Books, p. 64

2   Edited by William Zinsser (ed.), (1998), *Inventing the Truth: The Art and Craft of Memoir*

3   Elizabeth Bowen, (1945), 'Notes on Writing a Novel', Available from: NarrativeMagazine.com

4   Tony and Barry Buzan, (1993), *The Mind Map Book*, BBC Active

5   Chris Knight, (1991), *Blood Relations: Menstruation and the Origins of Culture*, London & New Haven: Yale University Press

6   Richard Dawkins, (1976), *The Selfish Gene The Selfish Gene*, New York City: Oxford University Press

7   Horace, *Ars Poetica*, (c.18 BCE), poetical translation by Philip Francis, ebook digitised by Google.

8   John Truby, (2007), *The Anatomy of Story*, Faber and Faber Inc.

9   Michael Meyer translation of *Ibsen: Plays Three,* (1980), London: Eyre Methuen, p. 288 in 'Note on the Translations'

10   Blake Snyder, (2005), *Save the Cat!*, Michael Wiese Productions

11   E.M. Forster, (2005), *Aspects of the Novel*, Penguin Classics, p. 73 onwards

12   In-Sook Chappell, (2009), *This Isn't Romance*, London: Oberon Modern Plays, p. 17

13   Hassan Abdulrazzak, (2007), *Baghdad Wedding*, London: Oberon Modern Plays, p. 39

14   Howard Jacobson transcript, http://www.open2.net/writing/howardjacobson.html

15   Kurt Vonnegut, (1999), *8 Rules for Writers*, Bagombo Snuff Box: Uncollected Short Fiction, New York: G.P. Putnam's Sons, pp. 9-10.

16   Viktor Shklovsky, (1998, 1917), 'Art as Technique' in *Literary Theory: An Anthology* edited by Julie Rivkin and Michael Ryan, Malden: Blackwell Publishing Ltd

17   No-Sweat Shakespeare website created by John and Warren King

18   James Joyce, *A Portrait of the Artist as a Young Man* (2008;1916), South Carolina: Forgotten Books, p. 198

19   Aristotle, (1999), *Poetics*, London: Nick Hern Books, p. 35

20   Roland Barthes, (1968), *The Death of the Author*, ref. to Nietzsche

21   Hassan Abdulrazzak, (2007), *Baghdad Wedding*, London: Oberon Modern Plays, p.102

22   Brian Logan, (2009), 'All the World's a Stage' interview in *New Statesman,* March 2009

23   Kenan Malik, (2011), 'Art for Whose Sake' in *Beyond Belief: Theatre, Freedom of Expression and Public Order*, published by Index on Censorship

24   Lisa Goldman, (2012), 'Silence One Story and Another is Born' in *Theatre Censorship Past and Present: Case Studies from Around the World*, edited by Catherine O'Leary and Mike Thompson, London: Routledge

25   Eg. Occupy London movement outside St Paul's (2011-12)

26   David Mamet, (2007; 1998), *Three Uses of the Knife,* London: Methuen Drama, p. 23

27   Toni Morrison, (1998), in W. Zinsser [ed.], *Inventing the Truth, The Art and Craft of Memoir,* Boston: Mariner Books

28   Arthur Quiller-Couch, (1916), *The Art of Writing,* Cambridge University Press, Chapter 12

29   Somerset Maugham, (2009), letter to brother, quoted in Selina Hastings, *The Secret Lives of Somerset Maugham,* John Murray

References

Referenced plays that I developed, directed and/or produced/co-produced

Abdulrazzak, Hassan, (2007), *Baghdad Wedding,* London: Oberon Modern Plays

Adshead, Kay, (2001), *The Bogus Woman,* London: Oberon Modern Plays

Agboluaje, Oladipo, (2009), *Iya Ile,* London: Oberon Modern Plays

Agboluaje, Oladipo, (2006), *The Christ of Coldharbour Lane,* London: Oberon Modern Plays

Bancil, Parv, (1998), *Made in England* in *Black and Asian Plays,* London: Aurora New Plays

Bhatti, Gurpreet Kaur, (2010), *Behud,* London: Oberon Modern Plays

Chappell, In-Sook, (2009), *This Isn't Romance,* London: Oberon Modern Plays

Goldman, Lisa, (2005), *Hoxton Story* (unpublished walkabout play)

Gupta, Tanika, (2007), *White Boy,* London: Oberon Modern Plays

Kelly, Dennis, (2009), *Orphans,* London: Oberon Modern Plays

Noble, Kim, (2009), *Kim Noble Will Die* (unpublished performance)

Langridge, Natasha, (2009), *Shraddā,* London: Oberon Modern Plays

Maslowska, Dorota, translated by Lisa Goldman and Paul Sirett, (2008), *A Couple of Poor Polish Speaking Romanians,* London: Oberon Modern Plays

Neilson, Anthony, (1998), *The Night before Christmas* in *Anthony Neilson: Plays 1,* London: Methuen Drama

Neilson, Anthony, (1997), *The Censor,* London: Methuen Drama

Neilson, Anthony, (2002), *Stitching,* London: Methuen Drama

Ridley, Philip, (2007), *Leaves of Glass,* London: Methuen Drama

Ridley, Philip, (2008), *Piranha Heights,* London: Methuen Drama

Upton, Judy, (2002), *Know Your Rights* in *Judy Upton: Plays 1,* London: Methuen Drama

Young, Justin, (2007), *Moonwalking in Chinatown* (unpublished walkabout play)

Young, Rob, (1997), *Obsession* (unpublished monologue)

Other referenced plays, films and prose fiction

Acker, Kathy, (1984), *Blood and Guts in High School,* London: Picador Books

Ali, Monica, (2003), *Brick Lane,* New York: Doubleday

Arrabal, Fernando, (1967),*Guernica,* London: Calder and Boyars

Beckett, Samuel, (2006; 1957), *Endgame* in *The Complete Dramatic Works of Samuel Beckett,* London: Faber and Faber

Beckett, Samuel, (2006; 1961), *Happy Days* in *The Complete Dramatic Works of Samuel Beckett,* London: Faber and Faber

Beckett, Samuel, (2006; 1963), *Play* in *The Complete Dramatic Works of Samuel Beckett,* London: Faber and Faber

Bennett, Ronan, (2011), *Top Boy* (Channel 4)

Bennett, Ronan, (1993), *Love Lies Bleeding* (BBC)

Bennett, Ronan, (2001), *Rebel Heart* (BBC)

Bennett, Ronan, (2004), *The Hamburg Cell* (Channel 4)

Bennett, Ronan, (2008), *10 Days to War* (BBC)

Bhatti, Gurpreet Kaur, (2004), *Behzti,* London: Oberon Modern Plays

Bond, Edward, (2000; 1965), *Saved,* London: Methuen Modern Plays

Bowen, Elizabeth, (2002; 1946), *The House in Paris,* New York: Anchor Books

Bowen, Elizabeth, (2011; 1929), *The Death of the Heart,* New York: Vintage Classics

Brahmachari, Sita, (2011), *Artichoke Hearts,* Macmillan Children's Books

Brecht, Bertolt, (1963; 1948), *The Caucasian Chalk Circle,* London: Eyre Methuen Ltd

Brecht, Bertolt, (1995; 1949), *Mother Courage,* London: Methuen Drama

Brecht, Bertolt, (1977; 1929), *The Measures Taken and other Lehrstucke,* London: Methuen Drama

Buñuel, Luis, (2007; 1928), *Un Chien Andalou (An Andalusian Dog)* [DVD] France: Umbrella

Capra, Frank (director and producer) et al., (1946), *It's a Wonderful Life,* USA: Liberty Films

Carroll, Lewis, (2007; 1865), *Alice's Adventures in Wonderland,* London: Penguin Popular Classics

Cartwright, Anthony, (2009), *Heartland,* Birmingham: Tindal Street Press

Churchill, Caryl, (2008; 1997), *Blue Kettle* in *Caryl Churchill: Plays: 4*, London: Nick Hern Books

Churchill, Caryl, (2008; 2000), *Far Away* in *Caryl Churchill: Plays: 4*, London: Nick Hern Books

Churchill, Caryl, (2009), *Seven Jewish Children*, [Online], Available from: http://www.guardian.co.uk/stage/2009/feb/26/caryl-churchill-seven-jewish-children-play-gaza [Accessed 20/02/2012]

Coney, (2009), *A Small Town Anywhere*, interactive, immersive theatre

Cortázar, Julio, (1991; 1963), *Hopscotch*, New York: Pantheon Modern Writers

Eco, Umberto, (2004; 1980), *The Name of the Rose*, New York: Vintage

Eisenstein, Sergei, (1984), trans. Gillon R. Aitkin, *The Battleship Potemkin*, Classic Film Scripts, London: Lorrimer Publishing

Etchells, Tim, (2009), *Void Story*, unpublished

Goldsman, Akiva, (2002), *A Beautiful Mind*, Shooting Script series, London: Nick Hern Books

Greene, Graham, (2004; 1938), *Brighton Rock*, New York: Vintage Classics

Greenhalgh, Matt, (2008; 2007), *Control*, [DVD], UK/USA/Australia/ Japan: Momentum Home Ents

Greenhalgh, Matt, (2010; 2009), *Nowhere Boy*, [DVD], UK/Canada: Sony Pictures

Fitzgerald, Scott, (1992; 1925), *The Great Gatsby*, London: Wordsworth Classic

Hare, David and Cunningham Michael, (2003), *The Hours*, [DVD], USA/ UK: Disney

Hosseini, Khaled, (2011; 2003), *The Kite Runner*, London: Bloomsbury

Hunter, Neil, (2007), *Sparkle*, [DVD], UK: Isle of Man Film

Hyland, M.J. (2009), *This is How*, Edinburgh: Canongate Books

Hyland, M.J. (2007), *Carry Me Down*, Edinburgh: Canongate Books

Ibsen, Henrik, (1981; 1879), *A Doll's House* in *Ibsen: Plays Three*, (1980), trans. Michael Meyer, London: Eyre Methuen

Ishiguro, Kazuo, (2005), *Never Let Me Go*, London: Faber and Faber

Kane, Sarah, (2001), *Blasted* in *Sarah Kane Complete Plays*, London: Methuen Drama

Kelman, James, (1985), *A Chancer*, London: Picador

Lavery, Bryony, (2009), *Kursk*, London: Oberon Modern Plays

Mantel, Hilary, (2009), *Wolf Hall,* London: Fourth Estate

Naphtali, Amani, (2002; 1990), *Ragamuffin,* London: Oberon Modern Plays

Naylor, Hattie, (2007), *Solaris,* BBC Radio 4

Naylor, Hattie, (2010), *Ivan and the Dogs,* London: Methuen Drama

Neilson, Anthony, (1998; 1993), *Penetrator* in *Anthony Neilson: Plays: 1,* London: Methuen Drama

Neilson, Anthony, (2008; 2004) *The Wonderful World of Dissocia* in *Anthony Neilson: Plays 2,* London: Methuen Drama

Neilson, Anthony, (2008), *Relocated,* unpublished

Nolan, Christopher and Jonathan, (2000), *Memento,* [DVD], USA: Twentieth Century Fox

Nolan, Christopher, *Inception,* (2010), [DVD], USA: Warner Home Video

Ontroerend, Goed, (2009), *Internal,* interactive immersive theatre

Orwell, George, (1977; 1945), *Animal Farm,* London: Penguin

Prebble, Lucy, (2009), *Enron,* London: Methuen Drama

Prebble, Lucy, (2011), *Secret Diary of a Call Girl: Series 1-4 Complete,* [DVD], UK: Warner Home Video

Punchdrunk, (2007), *Masque of the Red Death,* site specific theatre

Ridley, Philip, (2002; 1991), *The Pitchfork Disney* in *Plays 1,* Faber and Faber

Ridley, Philip, (2010), *Moonfleece,* London: Methuen Drama

Ridley, Philip, (2005), *Mercury Fur,* London: Methuen Drama

Rushdie Salman, (1998; 1988), *Satanic Verses,* New York: Vintage

Shriver, Lionel, (2006), *We Need to Talk About Kevin,* London: Serpent's Tail

Shakespeare, William, (1979; c.1606), *King Lear,* London: New Penguin

Shakespeare, William, (1978; c.1607), *Macbeth,* London: New Penguin

Shakespeare, William, (2000; c.1593), *Romeo and Juliet,* London: Wordsworth Classics

Sirett, Paul, (2004), *The Big Life,* London: Oberon Books

von Trier, Lars, (2000), *Dancer in the Dark,* [DVD]

Tarantino, Quentin, (2001; 1994), *Pulp Fiction,* [DVD], USA: Buena Vista

Truffaut, Francois, (2006; 1959), *Les Quatre Cents Coups (400 Blows),* [DVD], France: 2entertain

Tsiolkas, Christos, (2011; 2008), *The Slap,* London: Atlantic Books

Upton, Judy, (2002; 1998), *Know Your Rights* in *Judy Upton: Plays 1,* London: Methuen Drama

Various, *The Unknown*, unknownhypertext.com

Various, *EastEnders,* BBC

Various, *Cops,* BBC

Various, *Holby City,* BBC

Vonnegut, Kurt, (2000; 1969), *Slaughterhouse-Five,* New York: Vintage

Vonnegut, Kurt, (2000; 1952), *Player Piano,* Rosetta Books

Wade, Laura, (2010), *Posh,* London: Oberon Modern Plays

Walsh, Enda, (1997; 1996), *Disco Pigs,* London: Nick Hern Books

Walsh, Enda, (2007), *Walworth Farce,* London: Nick Hern Books

Welsh, Irvine, (novel 1996; 1993), *Trainspotting,* London: W. W. Norton & Co.

Welsh, Irvine, (1996), stage adaptation by Harry Gibson

Williams, Roy, (2007), *Days Of Significance,* London: Methuen Drama

Young, Rob, (2003; 2002), *Miranda,* [DVD], UK/Germany: 2entertain

Referenced non-fiction

Aristotle, *Poetics,* trans. Kenneth McLeish (1998; c.335BCE), London: Nick Hern Books

Aristotle, *Politics: A Treatise on Government,* trans. William Ellis (1912; c.335-323BCE), The Project Gutenberg Ebook

Camus, Albert, (1975; 1942), 'The Absurd Man' in *The Myth of Sisyphus,* London: Penguin Books

Campbell, Joseph, (1993), *The Hero with a Thousand Faces,* Fontana Press

Bowan, Elizabeth, (1945), 'Notes on Writing a Novel'. Available from: NarrativeMagazine.com

Dawkins, Richard, (1976), *The Selfish Gene*, New York City: Oxford University Press

Egri, Lajos, (1960; 1946), *The Art of Dramatic Writing,* London: Simon and Schuster

Forster, E.M. (2005; 1927), *Aspects of the Novel,* London: Penguin Classics

Horace, (c.18 BCE), *Ars Poetica,* poetical translation by Philip Francis ebook digitised by Google

Leonard, Elmore, (2007), *10 Rules of Writing*, New York: William Morrow and Company

Mamet, David, (2007; 1998), *Three Uses of a Knife*, London: Methuen Drama

Masters, Alexander, (2011), *The Genius in my Basement*, London: Fourth Estate

McKee, Robert, (1998), *Story*, London: Methuen

Naipaul, V.S., (2008), Rules for Beginners in *The World Is What It Is: The Authorized Biography of V.S. Naipaul*, London: Picador

Orwell, George, (2000; 1946), *Politics and the English Language* in *Essays*, London: Penguin Modern Classics

Shklovsky, Victor, (1998; 1917), *Art as Technique* in *Literary Theory: An Anthology.*, ed. Julie Rivkin and Michael Ryan, Malden: Blackwell Publishing Ltd

Snyder, Blake, (2005), *Save the Cat!*, Michael Wiese Productions

Truby, John, (2007), *The Anatomy of Story*, Faber and Faber

Vogler, Christopher, (2007; 1998), *The Writer's Journey: Mythic Structure for Writers*, 3rd ed., CA: Michael Wiese Productions

Contributing Writers

Hassan Abdulrazzak was born in Iraq and lives in London. His first play, *Baghdad Wedding*, premiered at Soho Theatre in 2007 (George Devine, Meyer-Whitworth and Pearson awards), was produced as a Radio 3 Sunday Play and also at the Belvoir Theatre, Sidney. His screenplay adaptation is in development with Focus Features. Hassan's second screenplay is *The Widow* (for NDF International). He works full time as a cell and molecular biologist at Imperial College. http://abdulrazzak.weebly.com

Oladipo Agboluaje Plays include *Early Morning, The Estate, The Christ of Coldharbour Lane, The Hounding of David Oluwale, Iya Ile* (2009 Alfred Fagon Award winner and shortlist Olivier Award). Short Film *Area Boys* and a number of feature films in development.

Rachel Anthony co-created and wrote *Mistresses*. Other TV credits include *Being Human* and under the name Rachel Pole *Bodie, Eastender, 20 Things to Do Before You're 30, Attachments* and *Black Cab*.

Steve Bailie has written numerous television scripts including episodes of *Primeval, Casualty, The Bill, Spooks, Red Cap, Soko Leipzig* and *The Transporter*.

Ronan Bennett Novels: *The Second Prison, The Catastrophist* (shortlisted for the Whitbread Novel Award, *Havoc, in its Third Year* (winner of the Hughes & Hughes/Sunday Independent Irish Novel of the Year award, listed for Booker Prize), *Zugzwang*. Non-fiction: *Stolen Years: Before and After Guildford* (with Paul Hill), *Fire and Rain*. Feature films: *A Further Gesture*, aka *The Break, Lucky Break, Face, The Hamburg Cell, Public Enemies*. Television: *Love Lies Bleeding, A Man You Don't Meet Every Day, Rebel Heart, Fields of Gold, Hidden, Top Boy*.

Gurpreet Kaur Bhatti Plays include: *Behsharam* (Shameless); *Behzti* (Dishonour), Winner of the Susan Smith Blackburn Prize 2005; *Behud* (Beyond Belief), shortlisted for the John Whiting and Index on Censorship Awards 2010/11. Screenplays include: *Everwhere and Nowhere* (2011), *Dead Meat* (Channel 4), TV drama includes: 9 episodes *Eastenders*. Radio includes: *An Enemy of the People* (World sevice), *Mera Days* (R3) and over 30 episodes of *Westway*. Currently on writing team for *The Archers*.

Stephen Brady TV includes *The Cops* and *Buried* (both won BAFTAS), *Silent Witness, In Deep, Vera* and *Taggart* among others.

Sita Brahmachari Novels: *Artichoke Hearts* (Macmillan 2011, Winner of Waterstone's Children's Book Award), *Jasmine Skies* (April 2012 Macmillan). Plays include: *Walk Along A River With Me* (2004), *Lyrical MC* (2007), *Arrival* (Tamasha, planned tour from 2012).

Laura Bridgeman trained as an actor at E15 and has an MA and a PhD in Creative and Critical Writing from UEA where she was awarded the HSC Scholarship. She has taught creative writing in UK prisons and universities. In 2011 Laura set up Hotpencil Press, publishing *There Is No Word For It*.

Published short stories include: *Gregory* (Brand Magazine, 2009) and *The Mustardseed Seduction* (Contains Small Parts, 2003). BBC Radio 4 play *Caterpillars* is to be broadcast in the summer 2012.

Trevor Byrne Trevor Byrne was born in Dublin in 1981. He is the author of *Ghosts and Lightning*, a novel, and co-founder of the Hyland & Byrne Editing Firm.

Anthony Cartwright has published two novels. *The Afterglow* won a 2004 Betty Trask Award and was shortlisted for the James Tait Black Memorial Prize. *Heartland*, was shortlisted for the Commonwealth Writers Prize (Eurasia), selected for the British Council Bookcase 2010-12 and adapted for BBC Radio 4's Book at Bedtime. His third novel, *How I Killed Margaret Thatcher,* will be published by Tindal Street Press in summer 2012.

In-Sook Chappell *This Isn't Romance*, her first play, won the 2007 Verity Bargate Award, was then produced for the Wire BBC Radio 3 and commissioned by Film 4. *Full* (B3 short film), *Tales of the Harrow Road* (community play 2010), *Hong Kong by Night* (BBC Radio 4).

Greg Dinner worked in development and acquisitions at several US Studios and also for Goldcrest Films, Allied Filmmakers and Carolco Films, heading drama development at RTE, Dublin in the mid 1990s. Screenwriting credits include: *Shipwrecked* for Filmkameratene/Disney, *The Matchmaker* for Working Title/Universal, *Stranded* for Hallmark and *Silent Witness* for the BBC. Currently working on a 13-hour series for writer/producer Lynda La Plante with EBTV. Greg has also lectured on screenwriting MAs in the UK.

Matt Greenhalgh Screenwriting includes: *Control* (nominated for BAFTAs in Best British Film category, Carl Foreman BAFTA 2008), *Nowhere Boy* (nominated for BAFTAs in Best British Film category). TV writing includes: *Clocking Off, Burn it, Cold Feet* and TV film *Legless*.

Tanika Gupta Stage plays include: *The Waiting Room* (National Theatre 2000, John Whiting award), *Sanctuary* (National Theatre 2003), *Hobson's Choice* (Young Vic 2004), *Gladiator Games* (Sheffield Crucible/Theatre Royal Stratford East 2005/6), *Sugar Mummies* (Royal Court 2006) and *White Boy* (*National Youth Theatre/Soho* 2007/8). She adapted Charles Dickens' *Great Expectations* (2011) for Watford Palace theatre and has written a new Bollywood musical for Sadlers Wells (2012). Tanika has also written extensively for TV and radio. She was awarded an MBE by the Queen in 2008 for Services to Drama.

David Hermanstein Screenplays: *Flipside* (Best Screenplay Award at the BFM Festival). Plays: *A Carribbean Abroad* (Manchester Library Theatre), *Safe* (West Yorkshire Playhouse), *The Healing* (longlisted for the Alfred Fagon Award). TV writer for *Doctors*.

Terry Hodgkinson studied painting at St Martins. He has written for TV and film for 30 years including 21 episodes of *The Bill*, 10 of *Lovejoy* and multiple episodes of *Midsomer Murders, All Creatures Great and Small* and many other TV dramas. Before screenwriting Terry worked on the production side of movies such as *Julia* and *The Go-Between*.

Lisa Holdsworth has been a TV writer since 2001. She has written for *Fat Friends, Emmerdale, New Tricks, Robin Hood, Waterloo Road and Midsomer Murders*.

Amanda Holiday studied art before moving into film – directing several shorts including *Miss Queencake* and *Manao Tupapau* for BBC /Arts Council. Her feature drama scripts have been supported by British Screen and Media II and been placed in the finals of international screenwriting contests. Between 2001 and 2010, Holiday was resident in Cape Town where she directed several educational television series. Currently developing a South African movie with B3Media and BBC Films.

Neil Hunter Films: Co-writer and co-director of *Boyfriends* (winner Best Feature, Turin Lesbian and Gay Film Festival 1996), *Lawless Heart* 2001 (Best Screenplay and nominated Best Director at British Independent Film Awards 2002 and Best Screenplay Evening Standard Awards 2002) and *Sparkle* (nominated Best Screenplay Evening Standard Awards 2008).

M.J. Hyland teaches creative writing at the Univeristy of Manchester. Novels: *How the Light Gets In* (shortlisted Commonwealth Writers' Prize 2004), *Carry Me Down* (shortlisted 2006 Man Booker Prize, winner of Hawthornden and Encore Prizes 2007), *This is How*, 2009 (longlisted Orange Prize and Dublin International IMPAC Prize). Short story: *Rag Love*, shortlisted BBC National Short Story Award 2011. www.mjhyland.com

Dennis Kelly co-wrote the award winning BBC 3 comedy series *Pulling*, 2006-09 and wrote the book for *Matilda the Musical* (winner of TMA, Evening Standard and Olivier Awards 2011). Other stage plays include: *Debris, Osama the Hero* (Meyer Whitworth Award 2006), *After the End, Love and Money, Taking Care of Baby* (John Whiting Award 2007), *DNA, Orphans* (Fringe First and Herald Angel Award 2009) and *The Gods Weep* (RSC). Dennis was voted Best Foreign Playwright 2009 by Theatre Heute. Radio includes: *The Colony* (BBC Radio 3 Prix Europa Award – Best European Radio Drama and Radio & Music Award – Scripting for Broadcast 2004).

Bryony Lavery Over 50 plays include: *Her Aching Heart* (Pink Paper Play of the Year 1992), *Last Easter, Frozen* (TMA Best Play Award, the Eileen Anderson Central Television Award, produced on Broadway where it was nominated for 4 Tony awards), *Stockholm* (Wolff-Whiting Award for Best Play 2008). *Kursk, Beautiful Burnout* (Fringe First 2011), *The Wicked Lady, Six Seeds, Smoke, Deadpoint, Precious Bane*. Radio: *No Joan Of Arc* (Sony nominated); *Velma And Therese, The Smell of Him, Requiem* and many classic adaptations including *Wuthering Heights, Lady Audley's Secret, A High Wind in Jamaica* and *Wise Children*.

Chris Lunt Lead Writer/Script Editor of the science fiction television series, *Empires*. Currently adapting *The Martian Ambassador*, writing science fiction movie *Dark Harvest*, television series *Prey* and *The Viper Code* in development for the BBC. Also working on a major motion picture with director Simon West and Michael Caine attached to star. Clients include BBC, Red Productions, Kudos, Hartswood, Leopard Films, Leftbank, E-Motion, SMG, Future Film Group and Prime Focus.

Stacy Makishi Her work is a cross-fertilization between live art, performance poetry, theatre, film and visual art. From 2007-10 she toured extensively internationally. Recent works include *Love Letters to Francis*, *The Making of Bull: The True Story*, *There's a Hole in My Heart that Goes All the Way to China*, *Around the Lunar World in a Day* and *STAY!* More on www.stacymakishi.com

Neel Mukherjee's award-winning debut novel is called *A Life Apart*. His second novel, *The Lives of Others*, is out from Chatto and Windus next year. More on www.neelmukherjee.com

Hattie Naylor was studying painting at the Slade School of Art when her first play was accepted in the BBC Radio Young Playwrights Festival. She has won several national and international awards for her plays and has had over forty plays, three short stories and an opera broadcast on BBC Radio 4 and/or 3. *Ivan and the Dogs* was nominated in the 2010 Olivier Awards for Outstanding Achievement. The radio version of *Ivan and the Dogs* won the Tinniswood Award for Best Original Radio Drama in 2009.

Anthony Neilson Plays include: As writer/drector: *Get Santa!*, *Relocated, God in Ruins, Realism, The Wonderful World of Dissocia, The Lying Kind, Edward Gant's Amazing Feats of Loneliness, Stitching* (Time Out Live Award 2002 and Herald Angel), *The Censor* (Writers Guild Award 1997, Best Fringe Play and The Time Out Live Award 1997), *The Night Before Christmas, Penetrator, Normal the Düsseldorf Ripper, Welfare My Lovely*. Radio plays: *The Colours Of The King's Rose, A Fluttering of Wings, Twisted*. Film: *Deeper Still* (short*); The Debt Collector*. TV: *Spooks*

Kim Noble is sometimes a performance and video artist, but is generally a bit of an arse. His multi-disciplined approach has led him to work across theatre, TV, film, art and comedy. Winning a Perrier award, being nominated for a BAFTA as well as Chortle Innovation in Comedy Award have done nothing for his confidence. His critically acclaimed solo show *Kim Noble Will Die* played to audiences world-wide. He sometimes posts things here www.mrkimnoble.com

Maysoon Pachachi has directed 9 documentary films, including the prize-winning *Iranian Journey; Bitter Water* about a Palestinian camp in Beirut, *Return to the Land of Wonders* about her return to Iraq in 2004 and *Our Feelings Took the Pictures: Open Shutters Iraq*. She has taught film directing and editing in the UK and the Middle East and in 2004 co-founded a free-of-charge film-training centre in Baghdad (www.iftvc.org). She is currently writing and developing a fiction feature film to be shot in Iraq.

Chris Paling Novels include *After the Raid, Deserters, Morning All Day, The Silent Sentry, Newton's Swing, The Repentant Morning, A Town by the Sea Minding, Nimrod's Shadow.* Chris was, until 2012, a longstanding producer of BBC Radio 4's *Midweek*.

Tom Palmer writes football stories for Puffin Books, including the *Foul Play, Football Academy* and *Squad* series. www.tompalmer.co.uk

Penny Pepper A genre-defying writer and veteran disability arts activist, Penny wrote the taboo-breaking, sexually explicit book *Desires* in 2003. She is currently looking to sell her novel *Fancy Nancy*, while working on her memoir *First in the World Somewhere*. She also works as a performance poet and occasional burlesque performer.

Lucy Prebble Plays: *The Sugar Syndrome* (the George Devine Award; TMA Award for Best New Play 2004 and Critics' Circle Award for Most Promising Playwright); *Enron* (Best New Play at the TMA awards 2009; nominated for Best Play at the Olivier and Evening Standard awards). *Enron* transferred from the Royal Court to the West End where it extended before touring and transferring to Broadway. Sony purchased the film rights with Lucy as writer of the screenplay. Lucy is also the creator of *Secret Diary of a Call Girl*, the hit TV show for ITV, which also aired on Showtime in the US.

Philip Ridley Screenplays: *The Krays* (Evening Standard Best Film and Most Promising Newcomer to British Film Awards 1990). Writing-directing films: *The Reflecting Skin* (winner of eleven international awards including the George Sadoul Prize), *The Passion of Darkly Noon* (Best Director Prize at the Porto Film Festival), *Heartless* (The Silver Meliers Award for Best Fantasy Film). Plays: *The Pitchfork Disney, The Fastest Clock in the Universe* (Evening Standard Most Promising Playwright 1992, Meyer-Whitworth Prize and Time Out Award 1993), *Ghost from a Perfect Place, Vincent River, Mercury Fur, Leaves of Glass, Piranha Heights* and several plays for young people including *Sparkleshark* and *Moonfleece*. Children's books include *Scribbleboy* (shortlisted Carnegie Medal), *Kasper in the Glitter* (nominated Whitbread Prize), *Mighty Fizz Chilla, Krindlekrax* (Smarties Prize and WH Smith's Mind-Boggling Books Award).

Paul Sirett Paul's work includes Olivier-nominated Ska musical *The Big Life* (with reggae musician Paul Joseph) at Theatre Royal Stratford East and West End, *Rat Pack Confidential* which also transferred to West End, *Come Dancing* (with Ray Davies) at Stratford East (Best Off-West End Musical, Whatsonstage) and Graeae's production of *Reasons to be Cheerful*. Other awards include: Pearson Award for Best Play, City Life for Best Production, New York International Radio Festival for Best Writer and Best Play and nominations for TMA, Evening Standard and Olivier awards.

Paula B. Stanic Paula grew up in Manor Park, East London. Plays include *What's Lost* (Alfred Fagon Award 2008), *Late Night Shopping*, co-writer of *St Pancras Boys Club*, *6 Minutes* as part of *Everything Must Go* (Soho Theatre), *Monday* (Red Ladder) and *Under a Foreign Sky* (Theatre Centre).

Edmund White Influential writer and literary and cultural critic, particularly on gay issues. Numerous awards and distinctions. Fiction includes: *A Boy's Own Story, The Beautiful Room Is Empty, The Farewell Symphony, The Married Man, Fanny: A Fiction, Chaos: A Novella and Stories, Hotel de Dream* and recently released *Jack Holmes and His Friend*. Biographies include*: Jean Genet*. Play: *Terre Haut*. Memoirs and autobiography: *City Boy, My Lives: An Autobiography*. Co-wrote *The Joy of Gay Sex*.

Roy Williams OBE for services to drama (2008). Plays: *Fallout, Lift Off* (George Devine Award 2000), *Clubland* (Evening Standard Award Most Promising Playwright 2001), *Sucker Punch* (Writers Guild Award Best Play 2011, Alfred Fagon Award 2011 and nominated for Evening Standard and Olivier Awards 2011), *Days Of Significance, Joe Guy, Sing Yer Heart Out for the Lads, No Boys Cricket Club, Starstruck* (Alfred Fagon Award, John Whiting Award 1998, EMMA Award 1999). Television: *Offside* (BBC BAFTA Best Schools Drama), *Babyfather* (BBC), *Fallout* (Channel 4 Screen Nation Award), *Ten Minute Tales* (Sky One). Radio: *Homeboys, Tell Tale* (BBC). Screenplays include: *Fallout*.

Rob Young Plays: *Crush, Tango 'til You're Sore, Suicide and Manipulation, Ex.* Monologues: *Obsession, Surfing, My Sky is Big, The Man with the Absurdly Large Penis*. Film: *Miranda, My Sky is Big*. Original screenplays commissioned by FilmFour, BBC Films, Sony, Working Title, Ruby Films, BBC1, Baby Cow, Channel 4. Radio: *Agent 52* (Radio 4).

Justin Young Plays include: *The Houghmagandie Pack* (Grid Iron), *Fierce: An Urban Myth* (Music by Philip Pinksy, Grid Iron), *Metegama* (Soho Theatre Commission), *August* (Music by Nick Powell, National Theatre Studio), *Moonwalking in Chinatown* (Soho Theatre). In 2007, Justin was chosen to be part of the BBC Writers Academy and has since written for BBC1 shows *Doctors, Eastenders, Casualty* and *Holby City*. In 2009, he became Consultant Producer/Head Writer of *Holby City*, and in 2011 he was made Series Producer/Head Writer.

INDEX OF NAMES

www.lisagoldman.co.uk